PART ONE: FLEEING

An intriguing and heart-breaking story of a strong woman forced out of her native Ghana by powerful forces. In a fluent and composed manner, Ewurabena gives us a unique insight into the culture and politics of a country where nothing is what it seems, and where the enemy is hard to distinguish from the friend. *Hague Girls Part One: Fleeing* will make you cry, smile, and think.

Rianne Letschert
Rector Magnificus, Maastricht University

The refusal by the State to honour a headquarters agreement signed by its own Foreign Minister and witnessed by a Supreme Court Justice is yet another reminder to the civil society in Africa of the unreliability of the governments they are working with … the principled and sober stand taken by Ewurabena and African Perspectives … against unprincipled attacks by the media is the enduring lesson of this great book … the first of the many to come … very soon!

Chris Maina Peter
Professor of Law Emeritus, University of Dar es Salaam, Tanzania, and Member, UN International Law Commission

Despite what those who slandered Ewurabena might want people to think, her captivating story allows the reader to see another image of Africans. Indeed, there are some among them who have great ambitions for their children. They raise them with dignity and with respect for others who have different customs, appearances, cultures and origins. This is why the Africans from this group remain dignified wherever they go and cannot conceive of engaging in racial discrimination. Ewurabena, during her studies at William Mitchell College of Law in Minnesota (USA), respected everyone but never considered herself inferior to anyone. This passage of the text is almost identical to my own experiences in western countries, in particular in Paris, where I attended the School of Magistracy, and in Phoenix, Arizona (USA), where I studied at the Arizona State University in the American English and Culture Program.

Reading the text made me proud of Ewurabena and I hope it will be read by many other people. Allow me to say that the experience with Dr Kofi and his opinion about apartheid is simply a pity.

I congratulate the author.

Fatoumata Dembélé Diarra
President, University of Legal and Political Sciences, Bamako, and Former Judge and First Vice President, International Criminal Court

This is a captivating story about the vulnerabilities of the personal characteristics of decency and integrity in a world where jealousies, personal animosities and self-interest drive agendas. It is also a story of the cowardliness of those holding authority and of political willingness to support smear campaigns. But more than that, it is the story of the strength of character of one woman who persevered in her belief in the rule of law to steadfastly right the wrongs that had been committed against her. In that respect, ultimately, this is the story of the triumph of Ewurabena's inherent morality and integrity as a human being over the moral bankruptcy of others.

Gabrielle McIntyre

Chairperson, Women's Initiatives for Gender Justice, and Chairperson,
The Truth, Reconciliation and National Unity Commission, Seychelles

Hague Girls is a book about courage and perseverance. It contains all the ingredients of a thriller: the intrigue, the machinations and manipulations of the media and government, the interplay of family and societal relations and the persistent struggle of one woman to challenge all of these factors.

But *Hague Girls* is a true story and not a work of fiction. This makes it inspiring, but also sobering.

It is the story of Ewurabena, a human rights lawyer and activist, and founder of African Perspectives, living and working in her homeland Ghana. It recounts the relentless attacks by the media and government to smear her reputation and destroy her organisation, and its attempts to stop her fight for truth and the rule of law.

It is a story about fighting back... but not alone. Fighting back by organising one's family, friends, community, professional colleagues, contacts – at home and abroad – in the struggle.

The reader is painfully aware that this is one story among the myriad accounts and struggles – in every country – about how the forces of power and privilege try to control the daily lives of people and then ruthlessly suppress peoples' intense struggles for equality and human rights.

The book analyses how white privilege is replicated across national boundaries: the author chronicles the 'Amy Cooper moments' in her own life, and the state-sanctioned police murders of black people, remembering George Floyd, Semira Adamu and others, and victims and survivors of apartheid regimes. She describes the still continuing struggle for gender equality, especially in international organisations which make 'paper claims' to equality. She recounts the discrimination and racism of foreigners towards the people in whose sovereign country they are guests.

The 'take away' from this book is that the struggles initiated by one heroic Ghanaian woman for her human rights *can* challenge the very foundations of the institutions and structures in her life. It is a struggle to hold government and the media responsible and accountable for their actions. It is a struggle for the core human values of truth and justice – which transcends cultural and geographical boundaries.

Hague Girls is a book which should be read, and then re-read, by anyone who is part of the struggle for equality and human rights.

Beth S. Lyons
International Criminal Defence and Human Rights Lawyer

This is a story that draws you in and keeps you interested. Ewurabena's experiences draw on the complex roles of identity, difference and gendered power relations. They show what can happen when one woman decides to stick to her convictions and play by one set of rules and then other rules conspire against her. The story explores the multiple, in-built and often petty ways in which society encourages us to conform and the difficult consequences for those who refuse to bow to pressure. Ewurabena's story is also about the love of a country, the importance of family and the frustration that comes from having to experience one's country as both an insider and an outsider. Well done, Ewurabena!

Carla Ferstman
University of Essex

For a doctor it may be very revealing to suffer an illness him- or herself. In Ewurabena's story, describing her awful experience, an international human rights lawyer has to suffer an attack on her integrity from a tabloid reporter. He did not reckon with her fighting spirit. With all her perseverance and strong feeling for truthfulness, she tries, come what may, to defend herself. Of course, she shows that she would defend and seek truth and justice for her clients too with the same persistency. This personal report carries the reader along on its quest for lawfulness.

Emma Crebolder
Acclaimed Dutch Poet

This is an intriguing story that will surely ruffle some feathers in Ghana and within the international community. The author was traduced by an investigative journalist of doubtful provenance, as it has now turned out, as part of an ordinary dispute before a court of law with an Accra landlady, when the perpetrators decided to play dirty.

In normal circumstances people with power in Africa tend to get away with this type of behaviour because those who have been wronged don't have the opportunity to put their case across. But not so in the matter of Ewurabena, a renowned international justice lawyer, who has told her side of the story for the first time. It's a lucid account of the underhand tactics, doublespeak and shady goings on that she encountered while trying to run a human rights organisation.

Apart from making her case, the author exposes, warts and all, the way in which foreigners flout Ghana's work permit system; discrimination at an international school in Accra; Barack Obama's unfortunate foray into the libel action taken by the author; the inconsistencies in Africa's human rights framework; and the rather dubious way in which donors deal with African NGOs.

A good read, indeed.

Desmond Davies
Former Editor of *West Africa* Magazine and currently Editor of *Africa Briefing* Magazine

Ewurabena, a human rights lawyer and indomitable fighter against all matters of unfairness and cruelty, becomes herself the victim of malicious attack, the target of a media smear campaign of fabrication and falsehood. The arrows are aimed straight at her identity both as a person of empathy and dignity and as the founder and leader of an international organisation dedicated to accountability and justice.

Told with the immediacy of oral history and reminiscent of the intimacy between long-lost friends, the story of Ewurabena is foremost a story of trauma, trauma's devastation and trauma's defeat. The reader soon hopes that no one will take advantage of the vulnerability that comes with the bravery of her openness.

Even as it runs like a brook and intermittently lights up with the glitter of irony and gentle humour, the narrative amounts to a tour de force. The large travel bag of Ewurabena's memories – memories assembled in different countries and cultures – have become weighted down by the grating granite stones of hurt, fear and fury. While she more than knows the experience of discrimination and more than knows how to cope with it, the misogynist assault on her personal and professional integrity is ballast unforeseen, difficult to counterbalance and vastly more crushing to stem.

Initially she pays no heed, dismisses the defamation as absurd, and underestimates the severity of the damage. Too easily she assumes that others have shared her fair-mindedness and backed her drive to fix what is crooked and right what is wrong. Before long her nonchalance is replaced by shock about the complot of beaks and claws of raptor birds whose feathers she had ruffled. Shock turns to worry about the likely impact of slander on her children. Ultimately her increasing anxiety grows to terror about worse things to come when new accusations arise, a distancing government hastily withdraws diplomatic protection from her organisation, and radio broadcasts filled with incitement to vindictiveness remind her of her dread during political coups of the past.

Still, she has her resources. Her inner compass may be rattled but it remains unbroken. She argues and litigates. She draws immeasurable sustenance from steadfast support by her husband and from the resilience of her children, from closeness with her perceptive mother and firm backing by her friends and relatives. She discerns in her dreams the continuing wise advice of her late father. She finds refuge. Count on her victories. Yet do they lift the weight from her soul? Count on her to continue standing up against the assailants of this world. Yet can she stop reliving the assault against herself? Can she stop ruminating about the instigators and motives behind her own nightmare?

The complex preparations for the funeral of her father, roughly a year prior to the defamation, may already point to the answer Ewurabena finds to free herself. The history and dynamics of her extended Ghanaian family offer insights into key aspects of the culture and customs of the country. The choice of the person leading the announcement of the funeral holds utmost significance. Ewurabena is adamant that it must be a truly fine person close to her father. One cannot help but hear in her insistence the heart-breaking dirge about her beloved father's passing. Much later she recognises that her opponents in the selection of the right person have become participants in the mudslinging against her. It now seems a secondary lament, beside the point. Instead it is her conviction about the importance of the right person for the telling about her father that has deep meaning and shows a symbolic parallel and a symbolic divergence: the importance of the right person to tell about Ewurabena. This time it must be She herself. And it is the reader acknowledging what was done to her and seeking to understand her suffering who may help her put the stones aside.

Jutta Betram-Nothnagel
Representative to the United Nations, International Association of Lawyers Against Nuclear Arms

This is an astute and searing depiction of a woman who spoke to truth to the ultimate power – the President of the United States of America – with a view to defending herself from libellous attempts to derail her pursuit of human rights in Ghana. 'We must celebrate daughters': Ewurabena's account should be celebrated, for its clear-sighted depiction of the multi-faceted structural forms of racism and gender bias that exist and obstructed the author on her path through the world, and for the empowering description of the author's strength and perseverance in transcending them.

Melinda Taylor
Lead Defence Counsel before the International Criminal Court

At the heart of *Hague Girls Part One: Fleeing* is a story concerning the targeting of women, particularly of colour, who occupy spaces previously reserved for men. Readers are introduced to the term 'media rape' which embodies the author's experience of being subjected to malicious stories in the Ghanaian press, all of which were subsequently perpetuated by various influential actors and powers. As if that experience was not enough, it is set against the backdrop of the casual discrimination faced by women and persons of colour in everyday settings – be it at school, medical centres, workplaces and even friendships.

Despite the gritty topics, the message from the story is uplifting – it is one of perseverance and striving for justice even when the deck may be unfairly stacked against you. The author is to be credited for baring all in such a personable and refreshing manner. She interweaves light-hearted moments and historical perspectives throughout, making her individual life experiences truly accessible to the reader.

Sarah Bafadhel
Barrister, 9 Bedford Row

I have known Ewurabena since our teenage years as cultural exchange students from Ghana to the Netherlands. I am deeply moved by the injustice she suffered in our motherland but equally proud of the bold and fearless woman and international human rights lawyer she has become.

I am glad she found refuge in the Netherlands, the very country in which we were both cultural exchange students many years ago when she was compelled to leave Ghana.

In reading this book the reader will be empowered to contend for justice irrespective of the status of the perpetrator they seek to hold accountable.

It is my hope that young African women will take inspiration from Ewurabena's story and continue to fight for justice for themselves and future generations.

Rev. Alexander Gyasi MBE
Founder of international educational charity Kingdom Lifestyle Mission,
Senior Pastor of Highway of Holiness church (London, UK), and
CEO of Highway House charity for the homeless (London, UK)

A beautifully written semi-autobiographical work with nuance and delicate layers, *Fleeing* brings perspective to a story once told in hushed tones in international justice circles. It raises important questions – even if not intended – about why evidence, not flight of fancy, prejudice, conjecture or power, must be central to justice. In telling her story, Ewurabena urges the reader to look beyond the surface, reflect and apply their minds. She does this in a way that draws you in and takes you on a journey across the world, from Accra to St Paul, to Accra again, and to other small and big towns in Ghana, to Maastricht, unnamed towns in Belgium, and finally to The Hague and the many places in between. *Fleeing* is, in fact, not a journey away, but a journey to (re)discover the truth. It is a solid attempt to right a wrong and to do justice where injustice prevailed.

Ottilia Anna Maunganidze
Lawyer & strategist, and Head of Special Projects, Institute for Security Studies

Hague Girls is a brilliantly told rendition of wrongdoing in West Africa with reverberations well beyond Africa's borders. It is about the pain and politics of wrongdoing avenged through the clarity of the narrative and the quest for human rights and the force of public opinion through the law. Well written in a lucid, clear, and creative way, Ewurabena offers a never-seen-before art form that will leave you wanting more. A must read. A tour de force!

Kamari Maxine Clarke
Distinguished Professor of Transnational Justice and Sociolegal Studies, University of Toronto

Ewurabena's story is emblematic of the complexity of human rights work – the professional and personal compromises human rights defenders have to make every day to achieve their goals and also ensure their personal integrity and safety. Her narrative is engaging and galvanising; every lawyer, human rights activist, and woman will find something to relate to in her story.

Alka Pradhan
Human Rights Counsel, Guantanamo Bay Military Commissions

HAGUE GIRLS

PART ONE: FLEEING

EWURABENA

#ChooseToChallenge

Theme of International Women's Day 2021

Published in the Netherlands (paperback)
and in Germany (hardback) in October 2021 as
HAGUE GIRLS PART ONE: FLEEING

This is a true story. It reflects the author's own experiences, observations,
and recollection of events. Some names and locations have been
changed.

A catalogue record of the paperback of this book is available at the
Koninklijke Bibliotheek, The Hague, the Netherlands. A catalogue record
of the hardback of this book is available at the Deutsche
Nationalbibliothek, Frankfurt, Germany.

Paperback ISBN: 9789464026627 (Boekengilde B.V.)
Hardback ISBN: 9783754307229 (BoD)

Paperback printed and bound in the Netherlands by Boekengilde B.V.
Hardback printed and bound in Germany by BoD.

ABOUT THE AUTHOR

A visionary, conceiver, creator, convener and an advocate, Ewurabena is the Founder and Director of an influential human rights and international justice organisation. She is a lawyer with practical and academic legal experience in Africa, Europe, and North America. She is the creator of the *Hague Girls* series, telling untold stories of intersectional discrimination in a globalised world. The stories are based on her experiences, observation of incidents, and recollection of events in her three decades of work as a human rights and international justice lawyer. The first in the series is her own story, *Hague Girls Part One: Fleeing.*

In memory of my parents

Elizabeth Esi Etsuaba & Joseph Kwesi Kumi

There is no greater agony than bearing an untold story inside you.

Maya Angelou, *I Know Why the Caged Bird Sings*

It's [your Personal Legend] what you have always wanted to accomplish.
Everyone, when they are young, knows what their Personal Legend is.

Paulo Coelho, *The Alchemist*

CONTENTS

1

TWIN CITIES

'ANITA, CAN YOU SUE PRESIDENT BARACK Obama for me'?

'Ewurabena, are you *crazy*? I can't sue Barack Obama, and you shouldn't either. He's a brother.'

I must have forgotten that Anita, like Obama, is from Chicago.

I told Anita about Obama's visit to Ghana and his shocking praise of a militant investigative journalist and tabloid reporter who had libelled and slandered me in the mass media not long before Obama's visit. In Obama's address to the Ghanaian Parliament – his 'historic message to Africa' – he praised the reporter, claiming that he risked his life to report the truth.

How could it be true that I was running a brothel? The truth is that the reporter was a mercenary who had been engaged to disparage me because of my critical stance on rule of law issues – a stance I often had to take after I moved with my family to Ghana.

Anita could not help but laugh when I told her that the reporter and his editor-in-chief had accused me in the media of running a brothel catering to a diplomatic clientele. 'I can tell you were a big woman in Ghana,' Anita said laughing. 'Let me write to Barack Obama for you.'

As if that would do any good. I told Anita that my friend Professor Leila Sadat had already written to Obama on my behalf and had received no response. I had also written to Obama myself, and to Secretary Hillary Clinton, with the same result. I later posted my letter to Obama asking him to retract his endorsement of the reporter on the website of African Perspectives, the human rights and international justice organisation I founded. The letter was reproduced on other communication channels. Still there was no response.

'He's quick to apologise for his mistakes. He apologised for coming down hard on a white police officer for arresting and handcuffing a black Harvard professor in front of his own house. Why don't you let me write to Obama?' Anita reiterated.

Anita was a big sister to me when we studied together at William Mitchell College of Law in Minnesota. William Mitchell was also the alma mater of Warren Burger, the former Chief Justice of the United States. We arrived in 1984, the year that saw the largest admission of black students. Still, there were only a few of us. Minnesota was white and most of the black students had come from other states.

Anita and I met shortly after we both arrived in St. Paul. I was twenty, the youngest student to be admitted to William Mitchell. Soon after we met, I remember going to the school bookshop together to buy some textbooks. I needed a law dictionary, and the shop assistant asked if I wanted Blacks. I just heard 'black' and couldn't believe that America was so racist as to have law dictionaries specifically for black people. Upon gaining admission at Mitchell, I received various letters of support from the Black Law Students Association. I got the impression that in America you're either on the black side or the white side, nothing in between.

'I just need a good law dictionary. I don't care whether it is for blacks or whites,' I told the shop assistant.

Anita was laughing and beaming with pride when she explained to me that Blacks was just a particular brand of law dictionaries. She loved the fact that I had spoken so confidently to the white shop assistant.

On another occasion, Anita also accompanied me to the school administrative office. I asked one of the members of staff where to pay my tuition. She probably was not really listening and told me to go and see Dean Brooks. Dean Brooks was the dean of students, and I didn't think he was the one collecting tuition, so I asked, 'Why do I have to go and see Dean Brooks?'

Again, Anita was beaming with pride. 'What did I do?' I thought to myself.

'Ewurabena, you should have seen how your pride showed when you said to the woman, "why do I have to go and see Dean Brooks?"'

I thought I had asked a logical question. Anita explained to me that the reason the woman in the administrative office asked me to see Dean Brooks was because she thought I needed to make a payment arrangement because that's what they expect from minority students. Instead, I just wanted to know where to pay the cheque my parents had written for my first semester, that was all.

There was another African American student who was not as kind to me as Anita was. The school's student housing office had arranged for me and Dorothy to rent rooms in the lovely home of an alumnus of William Mitchell and his family. Four of the couple's five children still lived at home. The oldest, also a student at our school, lived elsewhere and visited often with her African American boyfriend. He looked bi-racial to me, but in America any person with visible black origins was simply black. The youngest of the children was about to reach a milestone, and already knew who her prom date would be. The house had four floors, each stylishly decorated. The couple's only son lived in the basement apartment, and they rented the beautifully finished and furnished attic with large dormer windows to me and Dorothy at the very reasonable price of a hundred and sixty dollars each, with water, heating and electricity included. We could also hang out with the family in the common areas. They only had one rule: no boys upstairs.

The family was welcoming and made us feel at home. The first time my parents visited me in Minnesota, the couple drove me to the airport in their large automobile to pick up my parents and brought them to their home for welcome drinks, before taking them to their hotel.

Dorothy, my fellow lodger, was from Alabama. She looked and walked kind of wild. She also smoked a lot, which meant she always smelled of cigarettes, including her long, smooth, beautiful hair. She hardly spoke to me, and when she did, it was usually unkindly.

One Friday night, Dorothy's friend Cheryl, who was also at our school and would usually say hello and make small talk with me, had come to pick her up to go someplace and was waiting in the car with the engine on. I realised I would be all alone in that huge house for the night.

'Oh dear, I'll be here all by myself,' I blurted out.

Dorothy looked straight into my face and said, 'No, you'll not be home alone; you'll be with the dogs.'

I mentioned this to Anita. She was neither disturbed nor surprised. Rather, she responded with a smile, 'Ewurabena, don't you see? Dorothy is from the South and has been confronted with racism all her life. Now she's confronted with an African sister who carries herself with dignity and pride. Don't you see, Ewurabena?'

Well, not exactly. I imagined Anita too had been confronted with racism, but she was so kind to me. Besides, who was to say I had not encountered racism?

When I was seventeen, I lived away from home as a cultural exchange student in the Netherlands. I don't recall seeing a black person in the village where I first lived, or in the neighbouring town I moved to when I changed families. I was the only black person in the entire school. While the students and teachers were kind to me and had been prepared for my arrival, I did experience some patronising behaviour from seemingly well-meaning people. One student told me that some people would not want to be friends with a black person but that she was not like that.

On another occasion, I went to pick up my watch from a repair shop, but the shop assistant on duty would not return it to me even though I had a receipt. When I returned home without the watch, my host dad called the shop to find out what the problem was. The shop assistant told him they knew the address on my receipt and that there were no black people living there.

I had another encounter with a shop attendant who spoke to me condescendingly when he saw me enjoying a bar of chocolate I'd bought from the shop and couldn't wait to start munching. 'We brought that chocolate from Africa,' he said. The Dutch news had painful portrayals of Africa: skeleton-like children with protruding bellies, disease, and famine. Those representations were real, but they were not the full story.

'Actually, I am quite sure the main ingredient in the chocolate comes from Africa, most likely from my country. Have you ever heard of cocoa?' I asked the shop attendant.

'What is kaukau?' he asked.

'Chocolate is made from cocoa. Let's look at the ingredients for this chocolate.' I looked on the wrapper. Sure enough, cocoa was on the list of ingredients – and not just any cocoa, but cocoa from Ghana. 'To answer your question, without cocoa from Africa you would not be selling chocolate; and for your information, my country, Ghana, is the world's largest exporter of cocoa.' I wasn't even sure if that was exact, but it was accurate enough.

Those experiences did not bother me. Rather, I pitied their ignorance. I would go back home after my cultural exchange year all grown up and experienced, with stories to tell, including about the racial encounters. Isn't the whole point of travelling so that you can go back home? If you know that your experience with racism is only temporary, you might not internalise it.

Yet sometimes we are our own worst enemies, as was so well illustrated by a Ghanaian doctor who was doing a stint in the Netherlands during my cultural exchange year. My host parents, Emilia and Jaap Spring, had lived in Tanzania for three years and so Africa had become part of them. Tanzania and its people have that positive effect. Jaap, a medical doctor, had directed a regional hospital in Sumve, near Mwanza, South of Lake Victoria. Emilia, a poet, had studied Swahili while in Tanzania. The Springs once invited my compatriot, who was a medical doctor in the Netherlands, to visit.

During our conversation, the subject of apartheid, then in full force, came up.

'Apartheid is inevitable,' said Dr Kofi.

'What could he possibly mean?' I thought to myself. Emilia and Jaap laughed rather uncomfortably.

I had always been strong in my belief about equality and took pride in the fact that Ghana was the first sub-Saharan African territory to gain independence. I had seen the independence address of Ghana's first President, Dr Kwame Nkrumah, on video, and so admired him. I watched as he stood in the Independence Square in Accra, danced charismatically in his *batakari*, made a one hundred and eighty degree turn, waved his white handkerchief to the crowds and proclaimed: 'At long last the battle has ended, and thus Ghana, your beloved country is free forever!' He then continued dancing. Nkrumah observed that Ghana's independence would be meaningless unless it was linked with the total liberation of Africa. It is said that Nkrumah brought dignity to all Africans – in fact, to black people everywhere.

Emilia and Jaap knew my stance. I was not shy in expressing my views. I often had discussions on North–South issues with Jaap in particular. So frequent were the discussions that the family decided that Jaap and I would no longer sit across from each other at dinner, because we almost always spoke only to each other, especially about those issues. Jaap admired my stubbornness and perhaps my unrealistic vision for a world free of racism, bigotry and sexism. Yet here was an older Ghanaian man telling us that apartheid was inevitable. Was he confirming that blacks were inferior to whites and that Indians and the so-called coloureds a little less so?

However, when we were alone for a brief period, my compatriot changed his position. Suddenly apartheid was not inevitable. Rather, he told me he associates Dutch people with it. Indeed, apartheid is a Dutch word. I didn't expect him to tell his hosts that he associates them with apartheid, but to tell them that apartheid was inevitable? 'How could he belittle himself like that?' I thought. Was he saying that in a multi-racial environment there was bound to be a hierarchy of the races, as I would be confronted with years later at an international school in Accra? Or did he mean that, in times gone by, if a group of foreigners left their country to settle in another, they were certain to oppress the natives to secure their own position? Or was he just being flippant, judging from the way he flipped his position when we were alone? Privately, I wondered if my compatriot got ahead in life by such subversive acts.

As for Dorothy, I sensed that whatever was going on with her was deep-seated, and I was not about to make it my problem by letting her behaviour get to me. When my parents came to visit, I told them about my strange housemate. She was polite enough to come and greet them.

Dad said to Dorothy, 'When will you come and visit us at home in Ghana?' Dorothy gave a big smile. She glowed. I noticed how beautiful she was.

That night, when my parents went back to their hotel, Dorothy came to my room and sat in one of the two comfortable chairs. 'Ewurabena, I think I am going to take your parents up on their offer. I'll visit the motherland.' She stayed in my room for a while, and we had a pleasant conversation, and remained fairly friendly from then on. Whenever I cooked my famous chicken and curry, Dorothy was welcome to help herself. She'd often say, 'Ewurabena, you can take a little something and make something so delicious out of it.'

In my first year of law school, I got to know a girl called Jill. I remember how confused I'd been when she immediately introduced herself as Jewish. I noticed that she was fully blonde. Was I supposed to introduce myself as African? Surely she could see I was black.

'Nice to meet you, Jill. My name is Ewurabena. I'm a Christian,' I said.

I'd never before introduced myself as a Christian. I didn't know that being Jewish was controversial or political, although I knew about the Holocaust and World War II. Back in Ghana, my parents had a travel agency and had organised pilgrimages to Jerusalem for members of our Methodist Church, I guessed just as a Catholic would go to the Vatican. Church members who went to Jerusalem were presented with certificates giving them the honour to be called 'Jerusalem Pilgrims'. I was under the impression that Judaism and Christianity were two sides of the same coin.

I spent my first Thanksgiving weekend at the delightful home of Jill's parents, where she lived with her father, who was a lawyer, her pretty and thoughtful mother, and her brother. I imagined Jill's dad was a fine attorney because he was so charismatic. Thanksgiving was festive, like Christmas but without church. There was oven-roasted turkey, dressing, mashed potatoes, gravy, green bean casserole, and pumpkin pie. Their friends and family members came and went, including Jill's grandfather and his wife. Jill joked about the fact that she had been a bridesmaid at her grandfather's wedding.

Over Thanksgiving weekend, Jill took me to visit family friends and family members in their affluent St. Louis Park neighbourhood. I knew I was fortunate to be able to study abroad and to be invited by Jill's family for this special occasion. At the same time, I wished I could spend Thanksgiving with my own family. Sometimes I'd complain to my parents about how I couldn't go away for long weekends to see my family like some of the other students from out of state did. After hearing my complaints a few times, Dad said, 'Well, that's what you got.' And what I got was not bad at all. I got to know Ghanaians who had not seen their families back home for many years because of green-card issues. One of them finally visited after ten years and told me how much her mother had aged. I remember thinking that the sacrifice of living in the developed world was greater than the benefits.

Anita found me and Jill sitting in the school lounge one afternoon and came up to me all smiles. 'Ewurabena, you look lovely, is that a new dress?' She did not acknowledge my friend. She used to say that Jill and I were not friends, that we were just buddies. 'It won't last,' she'd say. Jill once told me she thought Anita was a racist. She said Anita reminded her of some black women who used to go to a restaurant she worked at as a waitress when she was an undergraduate. She said the women were mean to her, nothing she did was good enough, and they never gave her a tip. Jill had an ambition to find a boyfriend, to show up with at William Mitchell's social gatherings. Her ambition manifested, and we would soon drift apart. Another girl she had been friends with, a white girl, would later tell me that her friendship with Jill also ended after Jill found a boyfriend.

I was also quite impressed about how Americans were so free with their language. Our course on the law of evidence was taught by a judge of the Hennepin County District Court. The kindly, somewhat elderly judge decided that one of the lectures should take place in his courtroom in Minneapolis, to give us students a feel for the courtroom. That was exciting. I don't think I had been in a courtroom before. It was a privilege, and I knew I had to be on my best behaviour. We gathered in his courtroom on a Saturday morning. For some reason the judge decided to call on me to present the case that was to be discussed. I had read it and was well prepared. However, how was I supposed to use the obscene word in the case?

I proceeded to state the facts of the case, involving a suspect who had confided in his wife that he had committed a crime. He had burned down their neighbour's property. I simply could not bring myself to repeat the suspect's specific words, for that would be so disrespectful. Would that even be allowed in the judge's court? Would it be legal?

'John Doe told his wife that he had burned down something,' I began. After I recited the facts of the case, the judge set the discussion in motion, but first he needed to clarify the facts that I had recited.

'John Doe told his wife he'd burned the damn thing, right?' he said to me.

'Good gracious, how could an honourable judge use such profanity?' I thought. I did not respond.

'He said he'd burned the damn thing, right?' the judge repeated, looking at me.

'He said he'd burned something,' I said.

The judge must have realised there was no point in him trying to get me to use a curse word, so he proceeded to engage the class in the discussion. Later, my friend Elfreda said to me: 'Ewurabena, you were cracking me up when you recited the case, refusing to say damn.'

'Oh dear, that vulgar word again,' I thought.

During my parents' first visit to William Mitchell, they waited on a comfortable sofa in the far corner of the school lounge while I was in class. When I went downstairs to be with them after class, I found them surrounded by many of the black students, mostly mature students. My parents would later tell me that every single black person who walked through the lounge went over to say hello to them and have a chat. They said a couple of white students also went to say hello. A Ghanaian and Nigerian man had also gone over to greet them. I told my parents about the advice I received from my compatriot, who was in his second year. He'd advised me to keep my distance from black Americans because they were trouble. He told me I'd be better off making white friends. I have not forgotten my parents' response to that advice.

'Ewurabena, blacks in America have struggled to get where they are,' Dad said.

'If blacks had not fought for their rights, you, a black African, would not have been allowed to seek higher education here in America,' Mum added.

The African American students had fun chatting with my parents. Ebony White said she loved Mum's braids. Mum wore braids when she travelled because it was convenient and also showcased her identity. When I told Mum that in America braids represent black power, she was so embarrassed and almost wished she had not worn them because she did not want to offend anyone. I don't think Mum offended anyone with her beautiful, neat braids. Somehow, Africans wearing braids in America did not carry political baggage.

As Ebony and the others bid their farewell to my parents, Dad gave them his card and said, 'Let me know when you plan to visit Ghana.'

Ebony looked at the card, beamed, and blurted out the name of my parents' travel agency almost with joy: 'Black Beauty Tours!'

As for Anita, she saw my parents each time they came to visit. She would make a point of driving me to the airport to pick them up. Then, in the course of their visit, she'd take us all out for a meal, sometimes even for breakfast. But she never invited my parents to her home, even though she lived in a nice house. When I read Vernon Jordan's advice to African

Americans in his memoir *Vernon Can Read*, I felt he was speaking to Anita. Jordan advised his fellow African Americans to entertain more at home. He said the host need not go all out; all that is required is good food and good company. I could have told Anita this myself, though I would add a good, full-bodied red wine. After law school, Anita returned to Chicago, where she wears to the courts of Cook County the authentic kente shawl my parents gave her.

When I took Klaas-Jan, the man who would become my husband, to visit Anita in Chicago a year after we started dating, she put us up in a fancy hotel, complete with champagne. We visited her home and various sights together with Elfreda and Cheryl, friends from William Mitchell, who had also moved to Chicago after law school. Anita drove us around Chicago during our visit. She wanted Klaas-Jan to see the contrast between the decadent wealth on the Gold Coast and the poverty in the South Side, which he found striking, especially since the two neighbourhoods were not far apart. 'Klaas-Jan,' Anita said to my boyfriend, 'this is America; this is reality.' Sometimes I thought she was exaggerating. Like when she parked her car in the South Side and she and I got out from the front, but she would not allow Klaas-Jan, who was sitting in the back, to get out of the car. 'No, no, you can't come out!' Anita said. 'This is a dangerous place for a white guy – you should lay down in the back of the car so no one can see you.'

While we were in Chicago, we dined at a soul food place which served chitterlings, or pork intestines. Dining on waste parts of animals is not that unique. Chicken feet were my Mum's favourite part, with the outer layer of hard skin and nails removed. My paternal aunt liked to cook the stomach lining of the goat with its intestines. Grilled turkey tail, the butt of a turkey, was a local favourite in Accra, especially served with hot pepper and onion sauce. We had a kitchen garden at my childhood home in Accra and we enjoyed nutritious and organic plant-based meals. Accra is a coastal city, so there was plenty of fresh fish. My Mum also grew up in a coastal town in the central region. Fish light soup was plentiful in our home.

When I was about ten years old, we visited my paternal grandfather in the western region of Ghana. They killed a goat to commemorate our visit. The first meal prepared for us was *fufu* and goat light soup. My grandfather's portion was served in a separate room, with the 'most powerful' part of the animal reserved for the head of the household. I was stunned when I happened into the corner room and found him eating. On top of the *fufu* was the goat's penis.

I established warm and lasting friendships during my time in Minnesota. I got to know the Ghanaian community and the broader African society and became close friends with a girl from Tanzania. Thecla and I would later share an apartment together. Friends and acquaintances living in the Twin Cities would visit and we'd cook for them. I didn't succeed in learning how to make soft chapattis though. I took Thecla to Ghanaian parties, and she took me to East African parties. With our friends, we'd go to the various places in the Twin Cities that offered two-for-one cocktails and free food during happy hour and go dancing at the various nightclubs. We even attended a Miriam Makeba concert in Minneapolis.

Before I finished law school I started work as a law clerk at the Ramsey County District Court. There I became good friends with two of my fellow law clerks, Michelle and Dusty. Michelle's dad worked nearby and would sometimes take us to lunch. Michelle still lived at home and on a couple of occasions I was invited for Sunday brunch at her parents' beautiful home near a lake in St. Paul. Michelle has worked in legal publishing ever since and Dusty has now worked as a prosecutor for many years. I have fond memories of my time in the Twin Cities and have thought of Minnesota a lot since the police killing of George Floyd.

Several months after I was called to the bar, I relocated to the Netherlands, on the 31st of December 1989. I had been offered a position in international law and human rights at the Faculty of Law at Maastricht University. It was an opportunity for me to pursue my dream of becoming an international human rights lawyer.

After spending just over a decade away from Minnesota, I returned from the Netherlands with my husband, Klaas-Jan, in 2001 for my maternity leave. I had been back with him for short periods, but this visit was an opportunity to spend substantial time there. Klaas-Jan, a legal scholar, arranged a stint at William Mitchell during that period. I'd planned my maternity leave in the Twin Cities not because I was expecting twins, but because I wanted to eat bagels and cream cheese for breakfast, watch my favourite soap operas, and walk through the skyways to window-shop. Klaas-Jan had been surprised about the heated skyways and heated public car parks. 'No wonder America went to war over oil,' he said, jokingly.

By the time of my maternity leave, I had worked as a visiting research scholar in international law and human rights at Maastricht University, where I met Klaas-Jan – I had not expected to find a good-looking intellectual in this nerdy academic environment – had got married before eight hundred people in my native Ghana, had authored the first monograph on the African Commission on Human and Peoples' Rights during my tenure at Maastricht University, had founded African Perspectives, a human rights and international justice body with offices in Maastricht and Accra, and had been running it for five years. My six-month maternity leave provided a much-needed break. We arrived in the first week of September, just before the 9/11 terrorist attacks. Michelle, by now a mother of three boys, arranged for a fine specialist to help me through the remainder of my pregnancy. The specialist used to joke that someone must have been punishing us, for why else would we come to Minnesota when it was so cold, and the snow piled so high?

Our daughters arrived in November. Michelle, a Catholic, told me our girls were born on All Saints' Day. There was a strong team present with the specialist. Klaas-Jan was given a doctor's white coat with a matching cap to wear, which made him look like a member of the medical team. I felt so blessed to have two healthy, beautiful girls. And they'd grow up sure of a father's love, just like I had. I come from a matrilineal culture, and I wanted girls. Dad used to say, 'Dear Lord, please give Ewurabena two girls,' and so it was. The good Lord also knew I had a busy professional life, and so she gave me two at the same time.

My mother conferred the highest matrilineal honour upon me when she told me *wo ase ntreɛ*: 'may your line of descendants extend widely'. I do feel blessed with my fun, smart, gorgeous daughters and have much to share with them.

My parents came to Minnesota for the birth and were pleasantly surprised by the girls' good size. 'No wonder you were in such discomfort, they're relatively big,' Mum said when the girls arrived. From when I was close to seven months pregnant, I could not lie down, so I tried to sleep in a reclining chair in the living room of the apartment we rented in downtown Minneapolis. When she visited during my maternity leave, Mum spoke often about her own mother, who'd passed two decades earlier. She said that if her mother had been alive, she'd have insisted on coming to help me with our girls as she'd done for my mother when she had her own children.

My younger brother, Aboagye, visited us in Minneapolis from San Francisco to meet his nieces and to see our parents. My older brother, Kobi, who had relocated to Accra from the US years ago, went to our parents' house to tell the household that I had given birth to twins. When I spoke to him the next day, he didn't know the sex of the kids nor their names. Privately I wondered how he'd broken the news to our relatives. Surely they must have asked about the gender and names of the new additions to the house.

Thecla, then a mother of three girls, visited from Texas after my parents returned to Accra. It was simply lovely, just like old times. Klaas-Jan's mother also came to help. Soon after the girls' birth, we celebrated Thanksgiving and

Christmas with Michelle, her husband Joe, their boys, and their extended family. We also met up with Dusty. Our girls were baptised in St. Paul shortly before we flew back to the Netherlands. The late Charles Asare, a member of the Ghanaian community there, helped arrange the baptism at a church frequented by Ghanaians. Old friends and acquaintances attended, followed by refreshments at the church and then a feast on the rooftop of the apartment we rented. We were given lovely gifts, which we brought back with us to the Netherlands.

I was convinced at the time that I wanted to be a stay-at-home mother. I couldn't imagine being away from my girls for a full working day, and might have seriously considered quitting my job if I had not conceived of and set up African Perspectives myself, or if I believed the organisation was established enough to thrive. My time would be my time with my children, and I would start writing when they were big enough to sleep four hours straight. I would write for two and a half hours most days while the girls slept. Writing would fulfil me, and I would not suffer the indignities of raising funds for a worthy cause, 'bragging and begging' as it is called: 'Our organisation has done so and so, therefore could you please donate fifty thousand euros to our cause?'

I don't think I ever discussed my plans to be a stay-at-home mother with Klaas-Jan, but I did discuss it with Edith, a friend and part of my support system in the Netherlands. Edith's boys were in university and her husband's job took him to faraway countries often.

'Ewurabena, keep your job,' she told me. 'Children grow up so fast; soon, they'll not need you.'

I kept my job because it needed me. Klaas-Jan and I each worked four days a week for several months after we returned to the Netherlands, and the girls went to the crèche three days a week. I wept the first day we dropped off our children at the crèche. I was convinced that I was the only African mother who left her infant children in the care of total strangers. Help from family would eventually arrive from Ghana, and the girls continued to go to the crèche for part of the week.

We must celebrate daughters. Ghanaian intellectual James Kwegyir Aggrey's wise words speak to the significance of girls and women: 'The surest way to keep a people down is to educate the men and neglect women. If you educate a man, you simply educate an individual, but if you educate a woman, you educate a whole nation.' We should of course continue to educate men, including on gender sensitivity, because what we are striving for is gender equality and men should be part of this process. A man educated in gender sensitivity would not say of his female political opponent that she's likeable enough, like Obama said about Hillary Clinton in a 2008 Democratic presidential primary debate. Nor would he praise a reporter who was to stand trial before a court of a sovereign state – a serial libeller and slanderer who had spearheaded a chain of gendered smear campaigns against a human rights lawyer. I appreciate Obama very much, especially for having shown that with determination and preparation, many things are possible, including becoming the first black President of the United States with a name like Barack Obama. But I do have a story to tell, and tell it, I will.

2

OBAMA'S CHOICE

OBAMA'S VISIT TO GHANA WAS HIS FIRST TO Africa as President. There was so much excitement. America's first black president returning to the land of his ancestors. The choice of Ghana was seen as recognition of Ghana's commitment to democracy, having had five consecutive and relatively peaceful elections. Ghana is historic, the first country in sub-Saharan Africa to have gained independence. The country is rich in culture and tourist attractions, including its unfortunate history of slave trade and famous slave castles. Others were more cynical as to why Ghana was chosen. There had been a recent discovery of oil, and seventeen months earlier Obama's predecessor, George W. Bush, had also visited.

While in Ghana, Obama addressed the Parliament in his so-called historic message to Africa. In that speech, he made the dubious endorsement of Anas Aremeyaw Anas, a reporter Obama claimed reported the truth.

At the time of Obama's visit and endorsement, I had Anas and his editor-in-chief and publisher of a tabloid newspaper, Kweku Baako, in court in a much-publicised defamation action. Anas had spearheaded a series of smear campaigns against me, asserting that I was operating a brothel through a spa I had set up. He did so through a tabloid newspaper publication, orchestrated radio and television discussions and pronouncements, and a fabricated video. These were all reproduced on the worldwide web. Suddenly, many people got to know my name, not only in Ghana but also among Ghanaians in the diaspora. Prior to that, the public did not know who I was.

Obama further said in his address before the Ghanaian Parliament that 'Africa does not need strong men. It needs strong institutions.' I couldn't agree more. So why was he endorsing Anas, a militant reporter with ties to those in power, who is said to be revered by the police?

At the time Obama visited Ghana, my family and I had retreated to the Netherlands. While I had watched the Obamas' arrival at Accra Airport on TV, I did not get a chance to see his live address to the Ghanaian Parliament. I'd planned to watch it later. I had not been aware of his endorsement of the defendant until I had a conversation with my lawyer Godwin a couple of days later. When I spoke to him, I was sounding all excited about the Obamas' visit – and didn't Michelle Obama look so graceful as she descended from Air Force One, all smiles, arms bare, toned and strong? But then Godwin told me Obama had endorsed Anas in his address. I was in a state of shock. I could tell Godwin had been affected too. 'We're now fighting an uphill battle,' he said. If Obama had got involved, then the stakes were high. We would not return to Ghana.

I called my mother immediately after I learned that Obama had championed Anas. I spoke to Mum often from the Netherlands, but she had not mentioned Obama's endorsement. Like many in Ghana, Mum had been excited about Obama's visit and had tuned in to listen to his speech.

She heard what Obama had to say about Anas but did not know how to tell me. She was so pained by it when I brought it up.

A renowned criminal lawyer in the Netherlands was helping me explore various options to bring Anas and Baako to justice. When I told him about Obama's endorsement of the reporter, he laughed out loud, as if to say, 'Only in a banana republic'. I believe Obama only unconsciously thought of Ghana as a banana republic where he could make pronouncements on the character of the lead defendant in an ongoing case before the law courts. I don't think he would have done the same in a western country like the Netherlands, for example. Being on the receiving end of unconscious bias is a reality for those who do not represent the existing power structures, like Obama did. Unconscious bias and unconscious discrimination are a reality for many women – African women, Muslim women, women of colour.

About three months prior to Obama's visit, on the morning that Anas' libellous story was published, I received a call from a journalist at Citi FM. 'Madam, there's an article about you in the New Crusading Guide; it is not fair to you at all,' he said. It was the first time I was hearing about the New Crusading Guide because I still had not fully localised, five years after returning to Ghana. To be honest, I was not a fan of Ghanaian tabloid news because their stories were often preposterous.

Since I was getting ready to take the girls to school, I did not have time to speak with the journalist and told him I'd call him back. It was a long drive to the school. After I dropped off the girls, I decided to go back home instead of going to work. The story in the tabloid was the talk of the day. It was discussed on the radio, on TV, and it was all over the internet. I called Klaas-Jan, who was in the Netherlands, to let him know what was going on. As he knew, there had already been threats made against me, and I had decided not to give in to blackmail. But he could not believe that Anas and his editor-in-chief, Kweku Baako would actually write such a story.

'I know it's tough,' Klaas-Jan said, 'but don't worry, they'll be called to account, and they'll end up in jail.' I wanted to believe that. Knowing how worried I was about the accusations, Klaas-Jan decided to return to Ghana that same week.

My brother Kobi called expressing concern that my picture had been published along with the story. My Mum and I didn't speak on that day, however – it was all too painful. What was a mother to say to a daughter who had been so viciously attacked in the media in what very much looked like political violence? And how was a daughter to console a mother who was herself being treated for a critical illness while also mourning the loss of her husband?

I received many calls from other relatives, friends and colleagues. My friend Lillian rang me when I got home. We both had the radio on listening to the media accusations. 'This woman has done a lot of harm,' Lillian said, referring to Barbara Bonsu, the woman behind it all. 'Don't read the article, Ewurabena, it will upset you,' she added.

But Klaas-Jan had already gone online to read the article. 'Read it,' he urged. 'He was probably drunk at Barbara Bonsu's joint when he wrote the article. There's nothing to it.' However, I couldn't bring myself to read it. Klaas-Jan later paraphrased the article for me.

The story of Friday 20th of March 2009 was entitled: 'Diplomatic Sex Scandal Hits Accra; Porn Activities Caught on Camera; Diplomats in Ghana Involved'. The article discusses in general terms issues concerning sex tourism and pornography in Ghana. It includes pictures of naked women taken from certain websites. Against this background, Anas reports that a spa named Working Girl Wellness Centre was subtly operating a brothel and he claims to have caught on hidden camera an employee of the spa engaging in sex with a diplomat. He makes his claim by stating, firstly, that the owner of the spa is Ewurabena, who runs a human rights organisation, African Perspectives, and enjoys diplomatic status in Ghana; and, secondly, that the spa is patronised by diplomats. Among the aforementioned pictures that are included in the article is one of me, Ewurabena. Anas invited the public to view the video of the supposed sex scene at the spa on YouTube. The video turned out to be fabricated – but we'll get to that later. Anas also went around the various media houses to give them a viewing of the video and to spread his disparaging story against me so that those media houses would broadcast the story on the airwaves and publish it on the internet. The perpetrators also had their fabricated story circulated through the Ghana News Agency (GNA), a national news outlet with the widest network of correspondents of any Ghanaian media channel. The GNA has foreign correspondents in key places around the world and its main subscribers are newspapers and broadcasters. My name was repeatedly called out on the airwaves. The story was everywhere. My seven-year-old daughters would later see my name all over the internet. Kaakra even asked me, 'Mummy are you famous?'

There were orchestrated discussions on the radio and other media outlets that a brothel runner had diplomatic status in her native country. A radio discussion was dedicated to this, and I was told that an expert who had been called in had advised that the government should prosecute the persons involved. I called the so-called expert off air and asked him how he arrived at that conclusion. He told me he'd received calls from a couple of people who also demanded an explanation for his conclusions. He said almost apologetically that the media men had called him with a specific allegation and that he had not been aware of the background of the media chaos.

The article looked like a political attack, especially as all this was happening just months after President John Atta Mills' National Democratic Congress (NDC) government was sworn into office. Some wondered if I had been involved in politics. I had not. I run a human rights organisation, African Perspectives, which is independent, non-partisan and apolitical. As a hobby and because of my love of facials and skin care, I had set up a little spa, which I had named Working Girl Wellness Centre, and clearly there is not much political about that. Yet in Ghana 'politics' is never far away, since many people who do have political connections do not hesitate to use them to further their private interests. One such person is Barbara Bonsu, from whom Working Girl and African Perspectives had rented premises.

Barbara Bonsu had earlier sent threats my way through Anas and my friend Lillian. One month before the libellous article was published, Barbara Bonsu had called to inform Lillian that she had a video tape depicting sexual activities at Working Girl and that if she did not receive a certain amount of money from me within four days, she'd have the video published. She also told Lillian that the diplomatic status of African Perspectives was 'fake'. This was not the first time she'd made that allegation against our organisation, and we'd been compelled to inform the Foreign Ministry about her spreading falsehoods concerning our organisation's diplomatic status. The government of Ghana had in fact concluded a headquarters agreement with African Perspectives to enable the organisation carry out its work freely, without fear or favour.

A headquarters agreement grants immunities to the organisation and its officials for their official duties. Such agreements are typically concluded with intergovernmental organisations and exceptionally with independent organisations that are also established in other countries, operate under an intergovernmental mandate, or simply have a regional or international mandate. The International Committee of the Red Cross (ICRC) is an example of an independent organisation with an intergovernmental mandate. The Council for the Development of Social Science Research in Africa (Codesria) in Dakar, Senegal, for example, is an independent organisation with a pan-African mandate. It does not have offices outside Dakar but works with and through partners primarily in Africa and the Global South. Both the ICRC and Codesria have a headquarters agreement in the countries where their main office is established. As for African Perspectives, it is an independent organisation with a pan-African mandate. It was first established in the Netherlands, where it has had offices since, and then in Ghana, and is registered in South Africa where it works with its partners there and also on its own projects. Our organisation operates throughout Africa and has a strong presence in the human rights and international justice landscape.

Lillian, my friend, was related to Barbara Bonsu's husband, a high-ranking army leader, Lieutenant General Bonsu, through her late aunt, who had been married to the General and had a son with him. However, Lillian hardly knew Barbara Bonsu and was not on calling terms with her. Had the General given his consent to his wife to involve Lillian, perhaps as a warning to me that the attempt at blackmail was not just an empty threat?

Lillian phoned to tell me about Barbara Bonsu's threats, and then, a bit later, called back to inform me that after our conversation, she'd seen six missed calls from Mrs Bonsu, but decided not to return them. Why did Mrs Bonsu so urgently need to follow up with Lillian about her message demanding money from me? She must have needed funds urgently and thought she could obtain it by force, despite a pending court case between her and Working Girl.

Barely an hour after Lillian's call about Barbara Bonsu's threats, I got another call: from one Anas Aremeyaw Anas, requesting to speak to me about the spa. I referred him to my cousin Kofi and another lawyer, John, who were both handling the lawsuit Mrs Bonsu had initiated against the spa and gave him their numbers. I also told him that a friend had called to inform me about Mrs Bonsu's threats. Anas insisted on talking to me even after I directed him to the lawyers representing the spa in the suit.

I asked him what his interest was: 'Are you doing this in return for free bowls of fried rice and chicken at Barbara Bonsu's joint?' I enquired.

That was when he threatened me, yelling, 'Friday, Friday,' and hung up the phone. I guess he meant whatever action he would take would be done that Friday.

When I mentioned to a friend that the name of the journalist who had called me was Anas, she sounded frightened: 'Aiey, Ewurabena, Anas is wicked oo.'

Anas did not follow up on the numbers I gave him. My cousin Kofi, one of the lawyers assisting the spa, tried to call him several times, but there was no response. Later in the evening, I spoke to Lillian again, and she informed me that Mrs Bonsu had called to say I had spoken to her lawyer. Bonsu claimed I had informed her lawyer that she had disclosed to Lillian that she had planted 'evidence' at the spa against Working Girl. In fact, I had not spoken to Mrs Bonsu's lawyer. But I had spoken to her reporter, Anas.

Barbara Bonsu's joint in Accra is a social place for tabloid reporters, journalists and others in the media. These have been appropriately described as the Joint's Media Mafia. Working Girl Wellness Centre was located near the joint's premises. The entire compound belongs to Mrs Bonsu, who ran her joint from the same compound.

Sometime in 2008, about a year prior to the media attacks, my cousin Kofi, the lawyer, phoned me with surprising news. He had received a call from a justice of the Court of Appeal enquiring about the case between Bonsu and Working Girl, which was pending before an Accra High Court. The judge knew Kofi through family and wanted to speak with him about the case. I wondered why a justice of the Court of Appeal would take the initiative to get involved in a case before another judge. I asked Kofi for the judge's number and called him. I told the judge I'd heard that he had enquired about the case. He said a judge could intervene in a case if the parties agreed that the judge could mediate. I asked him if he would be prepared to go on record about his approach and he said he would. I further asked him if he would be prepared to recuse himself should the case proceed to the Court of Appeal; he said he would. Since I believed it was in the interest of all parties to settle the case, I agreed to an initial meeting.

We met at the judge's house shortly thereafter – myself, my mother, Kofi, Barbara Bonsu and her lawyer. During our visit, the judge was upset with one of his house-helps and spoke to him in a threatening way. I wasn't sure whether or not I was glad that Klaas-Jan, who was back in the Netherlands, had not been at the meeting to witness that. He would have been so appalled. The meeting with the judge was not too long after Dad's funeral and Mum was wearing the customary pitch-black attire of a widow in mourning. I had stopped wearing black because my sadness was affecting my daughters. Noticing Mum's clothing, the judge expressed his condolences before turning to the matter at hand.

His initial approach was conciliatory. Had Barbara Bonsu and I not known each other for some time? I thought this might work, until he said that Working Girl had made improvements to Bonsu's property, and that it was our choice to do so. It was not a reason to withhold rent when the dispute arose, he said. I had the impression that the judge was intervening not as an objective mediator but rather on behalf of the General and his wife. Indeed, Working Girl's withholding rent to mitigate or reduce its damages or costs for improving Bonsu's premises was the crux of the matter before the court. Working Girl had leased an unusable shell from Barbara Bonsu on a long-term basis. The premises had to be finished to make them fit for purpose. Working Girl installed floors, pop ceiling designs, a wooden staircase, windows, doors, WCs and other basics and finishes to make the premises usable, which was why the spa entered into a long-term lease with Mrs Bonsu, so that it could recoup its investment over time. The spa, however, was registered as a company limited by guarantee, a not-for-profit entity. In other words, any profit made would be reused for the good of the spa. This non-commercial form was chosen to avoid any potential conflict with my engagement with African Perspectives and its diplomatic status.

It soon became clear that we had made a mistake by moving into Bonsu's premises, because she liked to flaunt and make threats with her military connections. Since African Perspectives' premises, which we were also renting from Bonsu, had not required much improvement, we could afford to move out of Bonsu's place by giving her the required notice. However, the premises the spa rented were not part of the original structure but a new expansion at the edge of the building. The new expansion done under Bonsu's supervision was a basic construction – a shell that had to be completed with doors, windows, floors, ceilings and other finishes.

When she received African Perspectives' notice to vacate, she resisted with threats. She even approached some of my relatives – my half-cousins once removed – with whom she had an on-off friendship, and as usual threw in her husband's military stature: 'Because of my husband's position it would be best to avoid a dispute,' she's reported to have said. It was a subtle threat. I was actually surprised when those relatives tried to convince me that our organisation should not move because they had been quite sceptical when we first rented from Barbara Bonsu. 'You're improving her premises for her. She's benefiting from you,' they'd said. However, since they'd now renewed their friendship with Bonsu they'd taken her side and said we shouldn't move. I told those cousins that it was a professional decision, and we did move. Mrs Bonsu threatened to 'take the spa' as she put it. The spa's position was that she should reimburse it for the improvements.

Another issue that the spa had with Barbara Bonsu was that, sometime after it began its operations, Bonsu gave permission to one or more expatriate missions in the neighbourhood to station their security guards on her premises, presumably for a fee, along with goodwill. It was apparently not attractive to have too many security guards on the premises they were meant to protect, but Bonsu's nearby joint was a convenient location where they could be within easy reach. Many embassies, including the American

Embassy, were in a neighbourhood adjacent to that of Bonsu's joint.

The preferred location for the security guards at Bonsu's joint was at the very end of the building in front of a masonry fence right behind Working Girl. This was not even discussed with the spa; they just posted the security guards there. It became an issue when one morning the therapists noticed that there had been a break-in through the back window – the exact location where the guards were stationed. It would have been near-impossible for anyone to climb into the spa through the back window without the knowledge of the security guards. Fortunately, only one of the windows was broken and nothing of value was stolen. This was brought to the attention of Barbara Bonsu, but she did nothing about it. The spa incurred some costs fixing the window. Bonsu continued to allow those guards to be positioned behind Working Girl.

I also mentioned during the discussion with the judge that, when we rented from her, Barbara Bonsu had the habit of sending men in uniform to African Perspectives' premises even for routine messages. This I believed was her way of flexing her military muscle, as it were. And while her suit against the spa was still pending, she'd go to Working Girl with her supporters to cause trouble. This compelled the ladies working at the spa to file a complaint with the police against her. The police accompanied Seba, the manager of the spa, to Bonsu's premises and gave Bonsu a verbal warning. Bonsu's defence for sending soldiers was that these were people who worked for her, because of her husband's position as a general. The judge intervened and asked if I really believed that a person of the calibre of General Bonsu would use soldiers to intimidate. I thought that was a rhetorical question, so I did not answer. The judge then asked if I found his earlier utterances to his house-help problematic. I told him that as a matter of fact I did, given that he was a justice of the Court of Appeal with certain powers.

I felt disquiet after the meeting. I also didn't feel good about having informally engaged with a judge on a matter before another judge. After they told those scandalous stories about me, the perpetrators were reported to have made claims in the media that some judges had advised them to go ahead and publish. There is of course no indication that the Appeal Court judge had encouraged them to do so. If it was at all true that the perpetrators had been urged to publish by judges, it could have been any of them.

After Barbara Bonsu's threat and blackmail one month prior to the media assaults, Mum and Klaas-Jan advised that we move Working Girl out of Bonsu's premises. My friend Lillian said she'd help find a new place.

I told my cousin Kofi that I was planning to move the spa from Bonsu's place. 'Sister Ewurabena, call her bluff,' he said. 'Treat it with the contempt that it deserves.'

I also sounded out John, the senior lawyer representing the spa in the dispute with Barbara Bonsu, about her threats. He laughed dismissively and said, 'Democracy is catching up with us in Ghana.' I thought so too and did not think Barbara Bonsu and her co-conspirators would be able to make good on their threats. How wrong I was. The re-establishment of democracy was one of my considerations for moving to

Ghana when President Kufuor was elected after Jerry Rawlings' nineteen-year rule. I wanted to believe that threats by soldiers and persons with military and government connections were a thing of the past. John then added a remark that was quite unsettling: 'Dishonesty is our major problem in Ghana,' he said.

Seba's plea that we wait until we had found a suitable place for Working Girl and made it fit for purpose before moving was an important factor. She was the manager and heir apparent of Working Girl. She had been the childminder to our daughters since they were toddlers and had even come to the Netherlands for one year on an au pair visa to help out before we relocated to Ghana. Working Girl would be her reward for having taken such good care of our girls. She feared that if we gave in to the threats and closed Working Girl temporarily, that might be the end of it. I decided that we would move Working Girl, after finding suitable accommodation and making it ready. But we didn't tell Barbara Bonsu, for that would be giving in to her blackmail, with her threat to publish her procured video with fabricated sex scenes if the spa did not yield to her demands for money and vacate her premises. We would not negotiate with an extortionist.

The morning the libellous story was published, Mrs Bonsu, having anticipated the publication, led a group of strong men to the spa's premises, seized Working Girl and its belongings and changed the locks. I instructed John, the lawyer on record for the spa, to cite Bonsu for contempt of court. First, she left the country. John told me he believed she was fleeing from justice. But then her supporters convinced her that she had nothing to fear. Upon her return, she evaded summons and continuously failed to appear in court, until she was faced with the possibility of an arrest warrant being issued against her.

The Citi FM reporter who had first contacted me to ask about Anas' libellous article called me back to ask if I'd tell my side of the story in an interview. I agreed to do so. In the radio interview, I told the Citi FM journalist about the background of the dispute with Barbara Bonsu. I explained that African Perspectives used to rent premises from Bonsu but vacated after giving due notice. Bonsu had then taken it out on Working Girl because she wanted to get back at me, especially after her suit against African Perspectives was dismissed by virtue of its diplomatic status. We had brought the dispute with African Perspectives to the attention of the Foreign Ministry and had asked them to intervene in it or mediate. Bonsu then sought to evict Working Girl and subsequently filed suit, which the spa welcomed. However, she was losing the legal battle. I told the reporter that because the law was not on Bonsu's side, she resorted to threats and bullying while the suit was in progress, and eventually took the law into her own hands with the defamatory stories and by seizing the spa. I also told the interviewer on air that Barbara Bonsu's own lawyer once told me that I had no idea what his client had been urging him to do against me. Accra is a small place. I'd seen Barbara Bonsu's lawyer when I'd gone to an Accra circuit court to observe a case involving a human rights violation and had introduced myself to him during a break. By then he seemed to have lost interest in Bonsu's cases and had not contacted Working Girl or African

Perspectives for quite some time. He told me about Barbara Bonsu's lawlessness, which I knew about by then. The Citi FM journalist followed up on this lead in an interview with Bonsu's lawyer, but I am informed he dodged the question.

I later learned that my cousin Kofi had engaged Anas in a radio debate on the morning the libellous article was published. He asked Anas why, if his story was true, he had not filed a police report instead of going straight to the media. I'm told Anas responded that he filed a report with the police, but that is hardly believable, otherwise he would have volunteered the information himself. Besides, the police did not get involved at all. Everything was played out through the media.

Off air, after our interview, the Citi FM journalist asked me if I had not invited controversy with a name like Working Girl. Not at all. The perpetrators played on the name Working Girl because apparently 'working girl' means prostitute in some parts of the world. How misogynistic is it to suggest that a working girl must be offering sex in exchange for money! It says more about those who play on those words, using them to attack me in such a gendered manner. Only perpetrators with evil and depraved minds can make such a connection. For me, Working Girl stands for female pride and strength, something to cherish and strive for rather than to ridicule.

There is nothing untoward about the spa's name. In fact, my inspiration for it was the 1988 movie *Working Girl*, which is one of my all-time favourite movies and one I've seen many times. The story of Tess McGill aspiring to reach an executive position and how she was exploited by her boss

Katherine Parker spoke to me and my role with African Perspectives. While my position at African Perspectives is an executive position, and while I do not have any particular boss as it were, but rather a supervisory board, I too have felt exploited by some of the dignitaries I have worked with, just like Tess McGill was exploited by Katherine Parker in the *Working Girl* movie. I have engaged many high-level jurists and members of the judiciary with a view to helping them develop their awareness and skills on marginalised and undertreated areas of human rights and international justice and have purchased comfortable tickets for them to attend our international conferences and accommodated them in respectable hotels. An auditor once said to me: 'You know what your problem is? You put your salary on hold while purchasing expensive tickets for others.'

Many African dignitaries have learned and benefited from African Perspectives, but did they reciprocate when they were in a position to? Sometimes just the opposite. They enhanced their networks through African Perspectives' convening power and got to know of prestigious international positions thanks to their association with the organisation, which would all be fine and well if victims and potential victims had also benefited.

These days my focus is on empowering survivors and victims, particularly victims of sexual and gender-based violence, to participate meaningfully in pursuing their rights at national, regional and international levels. Victims and survivors of massive crimes ought to be seen and heard. In our beloved Africa, serious crimes are committed not only during conflicts but also in times of peace. Seemingly model democracies are in fact fragile and at-risk countries, a time bomb waiting to explode.

3

THE AMERICAN SCHOOL

FIVE YEARS PRIOR TO THE DEFAMATION, MY family and I had relocated to Accra, where African Perspectives had had a local office for some years. We moved there when the board decided to make the Accra office the headquarters of the organisation and the hub of its pan-African operations. We kept a small satellite office at the international legal capital of The Hague in the Netherlands, just in case. Would I have given in to the threats of the perpetrators if I had not had a Plan B? It is said that 'Plan B sucks', but perhaps not always.

Our girls attended the Roosevelt School in Accra. While the school was marketed as an international school, it was clearly an American-initiated and American-driven school. The US ambassador was a key stakeholder with the power to appoint three of the nine board members, with the remaining six elected by the parents. We also learned that the official address of the school was the American Embassy. Klaas-Jan had been sceptical and was not sure it would be right for our girls to attend. But then we'd visited the school with the girls. When we entered the school's gates, we were greeted by what looked like an Olympic-sized swimming pool off to one side. The grounds were well maintained. The girls looked very pleased, smiled shyly and walked contentedly around the grounds. When we got back home, they told Seba that they would be attending Roosevelt, even though we had not yet decided to put in an application. We also learned that the largest nationality groups attending the school were American, Ghanaian, and Dutch, in that order. Our daughters fit the bill, born in America to a Ghanaian mother and a Dutch father: the quintessential Roosevelt pupils. Our girls' enrolment at the school was also a full-circle moment of sorts: as a young man working as sales manager for Pan American Airways, my father had assisted some of the Americans who had been involved in the founding of Roosevelt.

About a year after our daughters' admission to Roosevelt, I joined the school board. I had received overwhelming support when I put in a bid to serve on the board and was duly elected. On the eve of the election, I was dining with a friend at a popular sushi place in Accra frequented by expatriates. I recognised a school parent who worked at the Dutch Embassy. We often said hello but had never really spoken to each other. This time she spoke to me from her table. She said she could tell that I was ready for the elections the next day. Indeed, the Dutch community at Roosevelt knew that I was the mother of Panyin and Kaakra van der Woude – the Dutch connection!

Earlier, when I sent in my statement of interest, I received a lovely e-mail from an official at the Danish Embassy. She had provided a grant for a judicial training that African Perspectives and the Ghana Commission for Human Rights and Administrative Justice had organised for judges in Ghana. I had not known she was a parent at Roosevelt until I got her e-mail. She told me she was glad I was running. She said the school had legal issues, and it was about time someone with a legal background like me joined the board instead of the usual diplomats, missionaries, entrepreneurs and industrialists.

Two outgoing Ghanaian board members also approached me shortly after I was elected. They complained about the American board chair who had repeatedly failed to accept the decision of the school board to replace the current superintendent, who they said was not running the school properly. They told me the elementary school principal was the one who de facto ran the school. I was also told the astonishing news that Ghana's Minister of Interior had not too long ago sent the police to the school with a van to arrest the many foreign teachers who did not have permission to work or reside in the country. Imagine the police walking into a classroom to arrest a teacher in the presence of their pupils. The superintendent had instead gone with the police to the police station. I later learned that even the elementary school principal was on a list of undocumented foreign teachers compiled by the school.

I didn't understand why the school and the principal were in that position. The school had been operating in Ghana for forty years, and the principal had worked there for several years. However, I believed the problem could be resolved, having already handled a similar residency and work permit issue for an American we had hired as administrative manager at African Perspectives. When she came for the interview, she told us her parents owned a communications company in Accra and had lived there for many years. She had joined her parents, settled in Ghana and worked for the company. My team and I had a number of meetings with her, including a lunch meeting. In the process she warmed up to me.

'Ewurabena, we have to talk about my residency permit.'

Why had I assumed that she had her permit? 'You've lived in Ghana for many years,' I said.

She told me her permit had expired and that a certain Mr Quaye often arranged her temporary renewals for a fee. She thought we could continue with that arrangement. I think she was worried about what could happen if she came clean with the Ghanaian authorities. I sought a legal opinion on the matter and was advised to write to the Minister of Interior. We followed the advice, and her stay was regularised, after she was made to pay a fine. It was that simple.

Perhaps I could help the school with its work permit issues too. I also wanted to understand how a school that had been operating in Ghana for forty years had found itself in this position, but this seemed to be a no-go area. The school principals got very defensive whenever the issue came up. They instead preferred to use their own approach. A white American parent was similarly defensive when the permit issue came up at a meeting between the parents and the board. 'It is not the school's fault,' she said abruptly. All the more reason why it should be resolved, one would think.

The school had other issues too. Some of the stories I heard about Roosevelt after joining the board had to do with outright racist behaviour and more subtle forms of racism. For example, there was the allegation that Les, a male Ghanaian outgoing board member, had assaulted a white female school parent. This supposedly happened in public during a parent-teacher meeting. Some of the parents who were present said no such thing happened. Nonetheless, Emily, the white American board chair appointed by a former US ambassador, wrote a letter to all the parents apologising for Les' alleged behaviour. This she did without consulting the school board. While Emily was appointed to the board by a US ambassador, her election as president of the board was a decision of the board members, not the US ambassador. Therefore, shortly after I and a few others joined the board, we asked Emily to resign from the presidency because of her conduct. She chose to leave the board altogether. Froukje, her vice-president, a Dutch woman who was married to a senior US official at the Millennium Development Authority, chose to resign too.

When I decided to run for the school board, I did not have any of this background information about the unsavoury events at the school. Our girls had barely been there for a year. My interest in joining the board was to meet my social responsibility in a time-efficient manner. Parents, especially mothers, many of whom had accompanied their husbands to Ghana for various appointments, were often expected to volunteer for a multitude of school events and projects, such as accompanying students on school trips or helping expatriate parents to settle in. Since I come from Ghana, I was expected to be hospitable. New parents would often tell me they had never visited a Ghanaian home. On two occasions I did the needful. I did not have time to be engaged in all these activities, so I thought the best way to make my contribution was to serve on the school board.

After I was elected to the school board, the school superintendent and elementary school principal tried to get into my good books in their own way. Six-year-old Panyin and Kaakra jointly received a school prize. When their names were called for them to come on stage, they looked into the audience to see if they'd spot their parents, and when they did, they smiled and waved to us discreetly. Later, Kaakra told me she thought all twins were receiving a prize, so they were surprised that another set of twins in their year had not been on stage. After we moved back to the Netherlands, Panyin told me she had been surprised to receive that prize. 'Were they trying to suck up to you, Mummy?' she asked.

In a similar vein, not long after I joined the school board, Seba, my cousin and the girls' childminder, was suddenly approached by the school. They asked her to cater a breakfast meeting. Although Seba had studied catering and had mentioned it in a conversation with the elementary school principal's assistant, the school had never asked her to cater anything prior to my joining the board. I felt that the offer of a catering contract to Seba had to do with my board membership and found it rather unsound. I asked Seba to decline the offer, which she did.

Upon joining the board, I was assigned to chair the policy and regulations committee to propose amendments to the school's constitution and bylaws. I found the framework of the documents to be adequate but in serious need of some critical fine-tuning. For example, the school's bylaws categorised and defined who would be given priority of admission if availability was limited. It looked like a classification based on a hierarchy of race and nationality. My legal eye saw unacceptable forms of differentiation. The categorisations were such that the practical effect was that Americans and nationals from other western countries were given first priority. Descendants of industrialists who had migrated to Ghana from countries like Italy, Lebanon and India had second priority. Ghanaians and others came last.

One of the board members, an American missionary, said that if she had come to Ghana to stay for a long period, she would not have minded her children going to a Ghanaian school, and therefore not being given first priority. I believed her because she's that kind of person – quite open and accommodating. Besides, there are many fine Ghanaian schools. Her point was that her family (like many expatriate families) would be in Ghana for no more than four years, and her children would be back in the American school system when they returned to the US. However, that was also exactly my point. An international diploma is convenient because Westerners and non-Westerners alike move around a lot.

Take Esi, who happens to be my friend. She's a Ghanaian, her husband Kojo is also a Ghanaian, and their three children are all Ghanaian. Kojo works for an international NGO and has been posted to a variety of different countries – Afghanistan, Mexico, Guinea. In 2007, he was posted to Sudan for three years. Sudan, a conflict-affected country, is considered a non-family area; therefore, Esi and her young children, who were already in the international school system, were given the option of living in either nearby Kenya or their native Ghana. They chose Ghana. After his tenure in Sudan, Kojo was likely to be sent to Geneva in Switzerland. Here's the question: who should have priority of admission, the children and grandchildren of industrialists who migrated to Ghana, or Kojo and Esi's full-blooded Ghanaian children? What about the children of US Embassy and agency officials: should they have priority of admission over Kojo and Esi's children?

My humble suggestion to the school board was to do away with categorisations and differentiations based on ancestry or colour. In addition to the bad optics, those differentiations did not serve any useful purpose. I believe that in an international school, priority of admission should be based on international need. So, if you were a Ghanaian, or of another nationality, and moved with your parents from country to country, whether because they were nomads or because they worked for an international organisation, then you would have met the standard of demonstrating an international need. But the powers that be did not like my suggestion. They came up with reasons to justify their preference for a hierarchy of nationalities. I found their resistance, as Americans, quite interesting because it is precisely these kinds of differentiations that multiracial and multicultural societies should frown upon.

When my family and I had to move back to the Netherlands in the middle of the school year, the international school in the city we lived in was full. Panyin and Kaakra's last name is as Dutch as they come – van der Woude – so they should have been sent to a local Dutch school, right? Wrong. They were given priority of admission to the international school because we could demonstrate an international need – not because their mother is Ghanaian, but because they were already in the international school system, having attended Roosevelt. My point was that people similarly situated should be treated similarly. So, all pupils who could demonstrate an international need should have been given priority of admission at Roosevelt, an international school. When international need is established, and the fees can be paid, the school should not limit admission based on race, nationality, colour, social origin or other questionable forms of differentiations.

As a human rights lawyer, I knew that the standard preferred by the Roosevelt school board and administration was unsound, even racist. Just looking at the list of categorisations made me sad. It was detailed and embarrassingly similar to how apartheid laws on the superiority of races were drafted, with a few exceptions. It is a paradox that in international communities, where you'd expect open-mindedness and tolerance, you sometimes find a subculture of bigotry.

On the residency and work permit issue, I was slightly surprised when a suggestion was made that the board invite the relevant government minister to dinner. How charming. I didn't know whether buying a Ghanaian minister dinner and offering a friendship of sorts would necessarily result in work permits, but I found the suggestion inappropriate. Instead, I suggested that the board request a meeting with the relevant state officials to address the work permit issues. I said it would be necessary to impress upon the authorities that the school was well-meaning. Then I suggested the unthinkable: 'What if the minister were given the right to appoint one school parent to serve on the school board?' The American ambassador had the right to appoint three board members, so why shouldn't an official of the host state appoint one? Or perhaps the American ambassador could appoint two and a Ghanaian official one. That way, the parents would still retain the right to elect six board members. For me such a gesture would be symbolic. It would show respect for the host state and a recognition that the school, although an international one, still had a relationship with the host state. It would send the necessary message of goodwill – but the board did not like it at all. Shivansh, the newly elected board chair, said that it 'would not fly', while the outgoing superintendent said that it would be a shame to politicise the school. Politicise? It was a well-intentioned suggestion. What about the American ambassador being entitled to appoint three parents to the school board – didn't that politicise the school?

The American school and associated communities were not the places to flaunt human rights ideals. An African friend in the Netherlands made this observation about my experiences at the Roosevelt School: 'Ewurabena thought she was just serving on a school board. She didn't realise she was dealing with American foreign policy.'

I was not on the Roosevelt school board to appease the powers that be. My main focus was to contribute to an international school where our children could thrive to become global citizens. I was also advocating for equal pay for equal work. I was of the view that while expatriate teachers should have their rent and other relocation costs covered, there was no reason why their basic salaries should be four times higher than those of their Ghanaian counterparts, who were similarly qualified and teaching multicultural students like they were.

Even my supporters on the school board did not share my views on this point, believing that it is just in the nature of expatriatism for foreigners to earn more than their local counterparts. That may be the case in the African context or perhaps in other developing regions, but it is hardly the case where the locals are European or American, and certainly not where they are in professional jobs. I of course understand that prospective teachers come to the negotiating table with different strengths and that a teacher from the US could command a better salary in her own country than her counterpart from Ghana or Greece could in their local setting. Generally speaking, an American expatriate teacher would have a stronger bargaining power. But should that result in such huge salary discrepancies? I had been surprised to see that Panyin's class teacher from the US earned close to double what Kaakra's class teacher from Greece earned. Our daughters were in the same grade, so my concern as a parent was whether one child was receiving a better education than the other. I wanted to understand the salary disparity. That too was not appreciated by the school administration. Moving forward, I believed it would be necessary to streamline the compensation package. Perhaps the Americans feared that I was a communist.

I had supported Shivansh, a Tanzanian of Indian origin, to become president of the school board, against the advice of a school parent I had become friendly with. He had known Shivansh longer and better and thought he was rather slick. But I had not heeded his advice. Perhaps I had been charmed by the fact that Shivansh had spoken our local language, Twi, to me when we first met. Shivansh worked for one of the multinational banks. After he became president of the school board, his interest seemed to have shifted, and he was keen to hobnob with the US officials. Shivansh became fast friends with Donald Teitelbaum, the newly appointed Republican US ambassador. Shivansh was elected by the parents, yet he was behaving as though he was first and foremost accountable to the US ambassador. I once told him that he was beginning to remind me of the previous school board president, who we had removed and who he had succeeded.

His response was notable: 'How could you compare me with them. Do you know what they have done?' He was referring to Emily, the former American board president, and her supporters.

'What could they possibly have done on a school board?' I wondered.

The day the fictitious article claiming that I was running a brothel catering to a diplomatic clientele was published, I got a call from Giselle, a Jamaican American board member I was friendly with. She was married to a Ghanaian, and they had recently relocated to Ghana with their children. I knew she was concerned about the racial tensions in the school because she had previously expressed her frustration that she had not moved from the US to Ghana to still be dealing with racism. I felt so comforted after Giselle's call.

'Ewurabena, I am so sorry,' she said. 'Ghana is not a democracy. In a democracy you have a right to a good name.'

Later, Giselle called to tell me that Shivansh had approached her. 'Have you heard the news? Ewurabena is running a brothel,' he'd said.

Giselle said she told Shivansh she did not believe that story. 'Ewurabena is a prude. Tell me Ewurabena has taken issue with someone, and I'll believe it, but not this story.'

In the days after the libellous article was published, when Seba and I brought the girls to school, I saw a Cameroonian woman who was married to a white American. We'd never spoken before but would give each other a smile and a friendly nod. This time she gave me a mean look. 'Seriously, did she think I would run a brothel?' I thought. Perhaps she was friends with the American board member who was married to a Cameroonian. Call me naïve, but the attitude of some of the white American members of the Roosevelt School, and by extension their allies, really surprised me. Why would they even be open to such a stupid story?

No one in their right mind would believe such a story. Only the racists and detractors accepted the lies or wanted to. I understand the discussions about the story even had a Dutch twist. There were conversations about the fact that I'd lived in the Netherlands and was married to a Dutch person, and that in the Netherlands they were quite easy about these things. After all, prostitution is legal there and the famous red-light district in Amsterdam is a tourist attraction.

However, like Giselle had been, others were sympathetic. I got an e-mail from a white American board member, saying she was praying for me. She and her husband were missionaries. We had not always seen eye to eye on how to resolve the school's issues, so I was touched by her gesture.

I had not heard from my favourite co-board member, Ngozi, a Nigerian American who worked at the US Embassy and had been appointed to the school board by the previous ambassador, Pamela Bridgewater, an African American. I called Ngozi and asked if she had not heard about the libel and slander against me in the mass media.

'What? No, I have not heard,' she said. Ngozi was clearly not part of the school's gossip circles, nor the gossip circles at the US Embassy for that matter. Ngozi and her husband, Emeka, bought the tabloid newspaper to read the story. She called later to tell me no clear-minded person would believe the story because it just didn't add up.

The media assaults continued unabated. Ngozi was so dismayed about all the fuss being made about me in the media and said: 'Ewurabena, you answer to a Ghanaian name and yet look at how you're being treated in your own country.'

Another school parent called to tell me she had overheard a corridor conversation involving some board members and other parents. Major Holly, a US army officer who had been appointed to the school board by the new US ambassador, had the tabloid newspaper with him. He had a dismissive attitude to the story because it did not make sense. However, he did say in reference to the article's author, 'He's a credible reporter though.' Major Holly would later tell me that Ambassador Teitelbaum told him he'd been informed that the subject of the much-discussed article was a Roosevelt board member and that the board should address it.

Giselle, my fellow board member, called to ask if I would meet with her and Shivansh, the board president. Giselle had been appointed vice-president when Tim, the previous vice-president, had lost his job with a US agency quite abruptly and was forced to leave the country. I remember how distressed Tim and his wife had been about their unplanned departure, with no concrete plans for a new job. Their children were in the two-year IB programme, and it would not be ideal for them to relocate. I had a conversation with Shivansh to find out if there was any way the school could help with the children's tuition, given that their father had just lost his job. I imagined Tim's employer paid the children's tuition and now he was no longer employed.

'Are you saying they shouldn't pay tuition?' Shivansh asked. He told me he had reliable information that Tim's children's tuition would be covered. I wonder from where or whom he got that reliable information.

Tim and his wife were said to be the bohemian type. Elected by the parents, Tim had been quite outspoken against the school's hiring practices. Several months later, when we were also forced to leave Ghana, Klaas-Jan would remind me that Tim had lost his job and been forced out of the country shortly after the Republican ambassador, Donald Teitelbaum, moved to Ghana.

At the meeting, Shivansh told me the school's 'stakeholder' was concerned about the article written about me in the newspapers. I told Shivansh that the story published in the tabloid newspaper was false, and that it had not been repeated in any of the national newspapers. Rather, it had only been reproduced in other tabloids and discussed on radio chat shows. In fact, on the day of our meeting, I saw an article in the *Daily Graphic*, the biggest national newspaper, calling upon journalists to be truthful in their reporting. I also told Shivansh I had sued the reporter and his editor-in-chief and that despite all their wild claims, the defendants were not cooperating with the court processes. The litigation and the defendants' non-cooperation had been reported in a newspaper that was closely following the case.

'If those stories were true, would the defendants rather not welcome my lawsuit to prove their case?' I asked them.

Giselle suggested that perhaps the school could send a delegation to observe the proceedings. Court hearings are generally public, so they would be free to attend. During the discussion, Shivansh kept referring to a 'stakeholder's' concerns. I understood this to mean that the American ambassador had taken an interest in the story. 'Stakeholder' was a term I had introduced to refer to the American ambassador in the school's policy documents.

I decided to write to the ambassador myself. I sent my letter to him in an e-mail attachment. Both the e-mail and the attached letter were entitled: 'Persecution of Ewurabena'. I informed Teitelbaum that I had initiated a suit for defamation against Anas and his editor-in-chief, providing some background to the case. Teitelbaum did not acknowledge my letter. One would have expected a response from the ambassador, given his apparent interest in the media allegations. I also called a meeting of the school board to address the issue. Klaas-Jan asked to attend the meeting too. The meeting took place at Roosevelt in one of their meeting rooms. Interestingly, with the exception of Ngozi, who was known to be my friend, the other board members appointed by US ambassadors did not attend. Shivansh, who had by now developed a close relationship with Teitelbaum, was present, so perhaps he was de facto representing the ambassador. Shivansh said there were concerns about what message was being sent to the children with a board member being in the media for such allegations. I made clear at this meeting, like I had done during the earlier meeting with Giselle and Shivansh, that those accusations had been made in a tabloid, and that none of the standard newspapers had repeated the story. I also told them we had not heard anything from the Ghanaian authorities about the story.

Indeed, not a single Ghanaian government official had questioned me or anyone working at the wellness centre about the story. Those who approached me did so in a personal capacity, quite upset about how I had been treated. Supreme Court Justice Sophia Akuffo called days after the story broke: 'Ewurabena, are you alright?' she asked. She told me she had just returned from a trip and had been informed about the story. She said she told those who informed her about the story that she had patronised the wellness centre, which the defendants' publication had described as a brothel, and that she did not believe the story.

Anna Bossman, the Acting Chairperson of the Ghana Commission for Human Rights and Administrative Justice, also called. She knew that I had set up a small wellness centre and she had previously expressed an interest in visiting it. However, she had quickly changed her mind when I told her the venue: Barbara Bonsu's infamous joint. Anna was a public figure and often in the media, not always by choice, so she preferred to stay away from Barbara Bonsu's joint, a favourite meeting place for Ghanaian journalists. As for me,

I was still relatively new in Ghana and, as it turned out, naïve about how things are done there. I had not known that Bonsu's joint was infamous. As far as I was concerned, I was not a public figure, and the media would have no interest in me personally. If I had been running a brothel, would I really do it under the noses of Ghana's media men and women?

In addition to my having informed the school board that I had not heard a single word from the Ghanaian authorities, I told them that the organisation I ran, African Perspectives, enjoyed a headquarters agreement with the government. Making that point was probably a mistake.

Ngozi told the board that this was probably a good opportunity to teach the pupils that not everything they read is true. Klaas-Jan told the board that instead they should really be supporting me against this injustice. Had they not seen all the good work I was doing on the school board, trying to sort out their legal issues? He believed firmly that if such stories had been written against him or a well-known white parent, the school would jump to their defence to say, 'Look at how unjust Ghana is.'

Interestingly, Giselle did not have much to say at the meeting. Was she not the one who had called to tell me that Ghana was not a democracy, and that in a democracy, there's the right to a good name? Was she not the same person who told me she informed Shivansh that she did not believe the story and that I was a prude? I was disappointed in Giselle, but not surprised. There are those among our people who'll express fraternity behind closed doors when people of colour are speaking amongst themselves but show another face when those representing the power structures are present, in order to get ahead. I understand. We must all make our choices.

The American board member who had sent me an e-mail to tell me she was praying for me when the libel first broke out was also present. This time she was not as charitable. She wasn't sure she agreed that I should remain on the school board, she said. I wondered whether Shivansh and the two board members appointed by the US ambassador, who were not present at the meeting, had got to her. There was no concrete outcome to the board meeting.

I recall something that Les, the former Ghanaian board member who had been wrongly accused of assaulting a white female parent, told me about the school shortly after I joined the board. He said some of the community members would organise sex parties where they had sex with whomever they picked through a lottery system. 'Imagine how horrific it would have been if I had attended one of those parties and ended up with Beth,' he said. Beth was a stern-looking and not particularly charming presence at the school. If such things happened at the school, it is no wonder that people within the Roosevelt community were apt to believe the brothel story.

A few days after my meeting with the school board, I was again attacked in the media, this time not in my personal capacity but in my professional one as executive director of African Perspectives. They woefully accused me of having fraudulently procured a headquarters agreement for the organisation. The media allegations went on to state that I constantly bragged about my diplomatic status and the accompanying CD licence plates. In fact, the diplomatic status was not personal to me: it was conferred on our organisation, although many people did not know that. As for the CD licence plates, many assumed it had to do with Klaas-Jan, simply because he was a foreigner. Only a handful of people knew about the diplomatic status of our organisation. And now I had shared it with the American school board. Mum had known about my wrangling with the Roosevelt principals and had had this to say when I called her about Obama's endorsement of Anas: 'Those people at the Roosevelt school had a hand in the attacks against you.'

4

COUP PRONE

THE SECOND WAVE OF THE MEDIA ASSAULTS began right around the Easter break. I had accepted an invitation to speak at an experts' meeting of Professor Leila Sadat's Crimes Against Humanity Initiative at the Washington University School of Law in St. Louis, where participants of Leila's meeting would stay on campus. The only time I'd stayed at a university campus in the US was when I visited my brother Aboagye in California, where he was studying for his undergraduate degree. He'd arranged for me to stay in Einstein's room. How cool was that?

I was happy to leave the noise behind me. I flew to Missouri with a connecting flight in Minnesota. While in transit at Minneapolis–Saint Paul International Airport, I thought about the many times that I had travelled through that airport. I remembered the day Thecla and I had flown out of Minneapolis–Saint Paul to JFK Airport to connect to separate flights – she was moving back home to Tanzania, and I was going to the Netherlands to take up a position in international law and human rights. We were both determined but not competitive.

I reflected on the course my life had taken. How had it got to this point – just because I had relocated to Ghana? A South African jurist that African Perspectives cooperated with had been surprised when she learned about my plans to move with the organisation's transition to Accra. 'Are you not scared?' she'd asked. Why would she ask such a question when she lived in Africa herself? An international justice icon I knew, also from South Africa, had stated bluntly that moving to Ghana would not be good for my extensive international justice activities. I thought about the friendships I had made in the Twin Cities. What would they think of the ongoing horrible events in Ghana? Somehow, communication with friends from different parts of the world had decreased when we moved to Ghana. However, Thecla came to visit and comfort me after Dad passed. And I was glad to have been living in Ghana with the girls and Klaas-Jan during the last years of Dad's life.

The morning after my return to Accra from Washington, I got a call from my office. They had just received a letter from an officer at the Foreign Ministry, now under the new government. The letter simply stated that the government was withdrawing our headquarters agreement with immediate effect and gave no reasons. Under the terms of the agreement, either party could terminate by giving six months' notice. This, the government did not do, in clear breach of the agreement. Macarious Akanbong, the officer who wrote the letter, had prior knowledge of the agreement before the new government was elected to office, as did the former chief director of the Foreign Ministry, Ellen Serwa Nee-Whang, who had left Ghana to begin her tour of duty as Ghana's ambassador to Switzerland in November 2008, months before the media attacks. I had had prior meetings with Macarious and the chief director about legal disputes our organisation had with Barbara Bonsu and one of the development cooperation agencies in Ghana. I had explained the nature of the disputes and our position that we were being bullied by General Bonsu's wife and the development cooperation agency and had asked the Foreign Ministry to intervene or mediate.

A meeting was scheduled for me and Barbara Bonsu to meet with Macarious at the Foreign Ministry. The date agreed upon just happened to be around the time when the upcoming presidential elections would be over. Immediately after the elections, Barbara Bonsu abruptly cancelled the meeting at the last minute without any proposal to reschedule. None of the presidential candidates received the minimum votes required to be elected, and so the elections went into a run-off. The predictions were that if there was a run-off, John Evans Atta Mills, the NDC flagbearer, would win. I could never have guessed at the time that the elections had anything to do with why Bonsu cancelled, but in hindsight I believe it was because of the run-off. While she was known to be a staunch supporter of the NDC party, I did not think that her husband was working with the NDC, because he had previously held a key position in the rival New Patriotic Party (NPP). Bonsu and her advisers probably realised that there was a good chance that her party would win, and her husband, the General, would be in the NDC government. They would then have an advantage over the legal dispute because in our part of the world political power trumps the rule of law.

Friends and colleagues outside Ghana were baffled about the extent of the defamation. 'How did the perpetrators think they'd get away with it?' a colleague in the international justice world wondered. Some asked if I come from an ethnic minority, and whether this explains the appalling way in which I was treated by Ghanaian politicians. Actually, I belong to the Akan majority, both from my matrilineal and patrilineal lineage. My ethnicity is also clear from my name. In any case, no one should be attacked because of their ethnicity. The barbarism I experienced was largely political. I am not affiliated with any political party and have always shied away from partisan politics. And even though I was pleased when Kufuor's NPP 'rule of law' government came into power after nineteen years of Jerry Rawlings' rule, I am not covered by Ghana's political patronage system.

The morning I was informed that our headquarters agreement had been terminated, Erica, a UK-based lawyer who owned a house in the gated community where we lived, stopped by. Erica and I had hit it off when we first met. She said the best *mpotompoto* – a one-pot meal of cocoyam cooked in palm nut broth – she'd ever had was at our home. Erica was in Ghana for the Easter break. She did not seem to be aware of the media assaults and I didn't tell her about them either. Erica and I were fast becoming friends and enjoying each other's company when she revealed her own friendship with Paolo, the developer of the gated community. I was surprised to learn about Erica's friendship with Paolo, because I knew she had once threatened legal action against his company. She had threatened to sue in the UK, where they both had resident status. Perhaps a suit against Paolo and his company in the UK was more threatening than a suit in Ghana, where they could manipulate their way through the legal system or unduly prolong the suit. Some other homeowners and I also had separate suits against the developer. The cases involved non-completion of houses, defective houses and land title issues.

As purchasers we had made investments in homes which had appreciated in value over the years. Yet we were confronted with title issues. Could we even call ourselves homeowners without a title deed or the promised seventy-year lease agreement? How is this even possible in a democratic country? Could we gain an advantage on our investments as the value of those homes increased?

I was friendly with a fellow board member at a development policy organisation in the Netherlands. We had been admitted to the board at the same time. He was head of the national pension fund in a European country, and I a director of a small charity. What did we even have in common? Our informal conversations involved the uneven distribution of wealth. I'd often ask him what a country like mine needs to attract investments and gain wealth. 'Basic things…' was his standard response. He was referring to things that are taken for granted in democratically advanced countries: peace and political stability, a proper functioning court system, checks and balances in the governance structures. I once mentioned the land title issues in the community where we'd purchased a home. 'Ewurabena, that story about your house is scaring the hell out of investors,' he said. But such lawlessness may actually attract certain types of investors.

African Perspectives used to have a project on human rights and business, with the slogan: 'Human rights are good for business!' However, I was intrigued by what an eminent human rights lawyer had to say during a roundtable conference on our project. Referring to the tiger economies, he expressed the view that certain restrictions on rights had in fact contributed to their economic boom. He also gave examples of major corporations that relocated their operations from advanced countries to poorer countries where they could get away with a lot. In other words, human rights may not be good for business. So, perhaps, Ghana's unfavourable human rights and political culture was good for Paolo's business.

After Erica became friends with Paolo and his close-knit family, he assigned their remaining twenty-six-year ownership of the site on which Erica's house stood to Erica and her husband. I am told he asked her if she wasn't worried about the twenty-six-year assignment. Paolo had promised a seventy-year renewable lease to the homeowners when he apparently only had a twenty-six-year assignment. I introduced a lawyer to the homeowners to find a collective response to the land title issue. The lawyer met with the homeowners and suggested that we collectively pursue arbitration. Paolo, who was earlier reported to have said that he could tackle homeowners one at a time, did not like that at all. I suspect the collective response I was proposing was not what he had anticipated. The suggested collective approach did not move forward, for reasons not known to me. As Erica's friendship with the developer grew, he apparently asked her who her friends in Ghana were. She said that when she mentioned me as one of her friends, Paolo had paused and said, 'Ewurabena, the lawyer? I am afraid that poses a conflict of interests.' Indeed, my cousin had warned me about my critical stance on the land title issues, which would have had huge financial implications for Paolo and his company if resolved. 'Ewurabena, please very be careful with those people,' she said. My cousin has lived in Ghana all her life and understands Ghana better than I do. She's a lawyer, but her advice was not legal advice. It was personal advice.

Therefore, while Erica and I got along, I was careful about what information I shared with her due to her friendship with Paolo. I did not bring up the libel at all, because Paolo, incidentally a Roosevelt parent, had surely heard. But apparently he had not mentioned the media stories to Erica. When she was about to leave our home, I asked her to say hello to everyone, referring to her husband and daughters. 'Who is everyone? Friends or foes?' she asked, laughing. I couldn't shake off the feeling that Paolo had had something to do with Erica's visit that morning.

Several months later, after we were settled in the Netherlands, I got a call from Erica. She had gone to quite some trouble to get my number. She had read about the libel and had also read my letter to Obama. 'Good for you,' she said referring to the letter.

The big elephant over our telephone conversation was of course her friend, Paolo. 'I asked him whether he had anything to do with it and he said he did not,' she said, referring to the media and political attacks.

'And you think he would have told you if he had something to do with it?'

'I am quite sure he had nothing to do with it,' she replied. 'He even said if you had gone to see him, he could have helped.' Seriously? Did he have any influence over the persons involved in the media attacks and the termination of the headquarters agreement? And why would he want to help? We were not friends but adversaries in a legal dispute.

For some weeks before the libel, I had repeatedly seen my deceased father in my dreams. Mum interpreted one of the dreams to mean that Dad wanted us to commemorate the one-year anniversary of his passing as custom requires. The reason we had not yet done so was because Mum had been in the Netherlands for medical attention in neighbouring Belgium. Klaas-Jan had stayed with her for seven months, while I remained in Accra with the girls, visiting the Netherlands during school breaks. We did commemorate the one-year anniversary of Dad's passing shortly after Mum returned, just a week after the brothel story broke. In one dream before the defamation, Dad asked me to call a high-profile person we knew who was revered by many and had media connections. That dream, which had seemed odd at the time, was beginning to make sense. The sudden termination of our headquarters agreement, coupled with the falsehoods and the uncertainty about who might have been behind it, was what triggered the urgent decision to flee.

Besides, I could not see how our daughters would thrive in a country where their mother had been branded a brothel runner and a fraudster. I told Klaas-Jan that I felt we should leave immediately. I would continue my work from the African Perspectives office in The Hague. Klaas-Jan had a tenured position in the Netherlands so there was no issue there.

I told Klaas-Jan that we needed to leave that night. I called my mother and my brother Kobi to tell them we would make arrangements to leave. I wasn't sure we would manage to leave that very night, but we would try. We made sure not to buy our tickets in Ghana, where everyone knew my name and face by now because my picture had been published along with the libellous article. I wondered if the publication of my picture alongside the fabricated article was meant to incite violence.

Klaas-Jan had been more relaxed about the incidents. Initially, he thought we were just having a moment of Ghana drama. However, the abrupt termination of the headquarters agreement, along with the government's dishonesty that the agreement had been fraudulently procured, gave him pause for thought. As for me, I felt that danger was imminent, having lost the protection of the headquarters agreement so suddenly and based on untruths. I was also concerned that the perpetrators had chosen first to attack through the print media and then the airwaves as they had done in order to gain public support for any subsequent planned government action.

Maybe it was because I grew up in a country where media disorder and political mayhem were intertwined. In my youth, to stage a successful coup d'état, the coup plotters had to seize the Ghana Broadcasting Cooperation and quite naturally Burma Camp, the headquarters of the Ghana Armed Forces. They would then make their announcement on the airwaves that the government had been overthrown. I was seven years old when Colonel Acheampong overthrew the democratically elected government of Dr Busia while he was in Britain for medical attention. I remember that I was standing in front of the sound system in our living room when, having taken over the airwaves, Acheampong announced that Busia had been removed from office. His was widely believed to be a bloodless coup. Acheampong was subsequently ousted in a non-violent palace coup by Lt General Akuffo. There were jokes that Akuffo walked into Acheampong's workroom one day, gave him a respectful salute and said, 'This is the last time I am saluting you,' to which Acheampong responded, 'My God!'

The June Fourth 1979 Revolution that brought Jerry John Rawlings into power and its resultant upheaval has stayed with me for a long time. As with Acheampong's coup, I was standing in front of the sound system in our living room when Rawlings made his announcement after his men took control of the airwaves. Within three weeks, all three former heads of state and several other high-ranking military officials were executed by firing squad after quick trials. There was widespread unrest among the population. People were divided on the executions. Those in favour chanted, 'Let the blood flow.' Rawlings was compelled to respect the ongoing process of a multi-party election and handed over to a democratically elected civilian president, Dr Hilla Limann, three months later, only to seize power again fifteen months after that, on the 31st of December 1981. This time he called his coup a holy war. At the time, I was a cultural exchange student in the Netherlands. I could not reach my family in Ghana, and they could not reach me. Eventually my parents' call came through and I was relieved that they were all well.

Six months into Rawlings' new regime, three High Court judges, including a woman, and a retired army officer were abducted and killed; their charred bodies were found shortly thereafter. It was reported that they had rendered decisions and taken actions that were not favourable to Rawlings' previous government and one of his new government officials. The decisions the slain judges had taken included the freeing of dozens of prisoners convicted during Rawlings' first regime.

There were several abortive coups during Rawlings' long military rule. One of them initially appeared to have been successful. The leader of the rebellion, Lance Corporal Carlos Halidu Giwa, seized the airwaves for some hours, repeatedly calling on Rawlings and his men to surrender. By then I had returned to Ghana from my cultural exchange year in the Netherlands and listened to the sound system in our living room, as I had done when Rawlings first came into power in 1979 and when Acheampong staged his coup in 1972. It appeared Giwa's message had been recorded. I was relieved to see my parents return home. They had been going to church, but quickly turned back when they heard about the coup. Giwa's message calling on Rawlings and his men to surrender went on. 'Where was Rawlings?' we wondered. As we stood in front of the sound system, a sudden announcement came from a panting Captain Courage Quashigah along the following lines, as reported by media outlets: 'At about three AM this morning, a small group of dissidents managed to force their way into our national studio and made a false announcement to disrupt the activities of the Provisional National Defence Council. I Captain Courage Quashigah, on behalf of the PNDC, want to assure the nation that the situation is under control and that those dissidents should report themselves to the nearest police station – or anyone seen in a tracksuit entering a military installation should be fired at on sight.'

Rawlings' military regime continued until the adoption of the 1992 Constitution, which established Ghana's Fourth Republic. Rawlings ran for president twice, serving the maximum two four-year terms as first president under the Fourth Republic. In total, Rawlings ruled for nineteen years, making him the longest-serving political leader in Ghana's history. It is said that Jerry Rawlings swapped khaki, worn by soldiers, for kente, typically worn by Akan royalty.

The 1979 firing squad executions happened at a place on the way to my childhood home at the Teshie Nungua Estates. We drove past there when we went to the city, to church, to our parents' office, to our primary school – when we went practically anywhere outside our neighbourhood. It is difficult to tell whether the corruption allegations levelled against the former military leaders were real or imagined because the trials were hurried, and the executions summarily carried out.

The head of state Rawlings overthrew was Lt General Akuffo. He was among the three former heads of state who were executed. I knew his daughters: we had attended the same primary school before their father became head of state. There were other children in our school whose parents were also executed. While in primary school, my siblings and I attended the birthday party of General Akuffo's daughter at their official residence. Her dad joined us at some point and cracked jokes and made us all laugh. General Akuffo's daughters also attended a birthday party at our house with their little brother after we finished primary school and went to different secondary schools. A few days before the party, one of our neighbours said he had noticed that the vicinity of our house was being patrolled. I remember thinking it was interesting.

I have a vivid recollection of a primary school function attended by parents and pupils. When the national anthem played, General Akuffo, who was seated on stage in his military attire with other dignitaries, did what he was supposed to do. He stood up like we were all required to, raised his right hand to the right side of his forehead, and stood tall, erect and still, like a handsome statue, in a perfect salute, while the national anthem played: *God bless our homeland Ghana and make our nation great and strong. Bold to defend forever the cause of Freedom and of Right; fill our hearts with true humility, make us cherish fearless honesty, and help us to resist oppressors' rule, with all our will and might for evermore.*

I was feeling quite sombre on the afternoon of the 12th of November 2020, my mother's birthday, when a journalist friend in London sent me a message stating that Rawlings had died. I had received a similar message three years earlier from an acquaintance in the Netherlands – but this message from a reputable journalist had to be true. I called home immediately. Why hadn't anyone told me? They had just found out themselves.

I thought about General Akuffo's children: the older girls, their little brother who was very young when his father was executed, the son who came after the older girls, and the twin toddlers the older daughters brought to our house just months after their father's demise.

'Who are these cute little girls?' I asked.

'Don't you know we have a stepmother living down the street from you?' the second daughter said. I'd heard the rumours but had taken them with a pinch of salt. Those twin toddlers would never know their father. I thought about my mother, who didn't come out to say hello to the Akuffo girls. She just could not bear to see them so soon after what had happened to their father.

Rawlings too was a family man who had only recently buried his centenarian mother. I felt sorry for his wife and children. President Akufo-Addo announced that Rawlings would be given a state burial. He further declared seven days of national mourning, and for all national flags to fly at half-mast. He acknowledged that he had long had a tempestuous relationship with Rawlings, but in the end they had found value in each other. We do not know how Rawlings will go down in history. I am reminded of what Professor Ali Mazrui observed at African Perspectives' inaugural lecture in Accra some time ago: 'Jerry Rawlings came into power a brutal dictator, and left office a democratic statesman.'

Thoughts of how the media was used to announce political upheavals in the coup-prone Ghana I grew up in went through my mind when the brothel allegations erupted. The subsequent hasty termination of our headquarters agreement was an indication that the government or its protected officials were involved in the smear campaign and media attacks. Rawlings' NDC party had been duly elected, and his former vice-president, Professor John Evans Atta Mills, a man of peace, was the new president. However, many feared the ailing president was not in control of his government. Armoured vehicles patrolled the streets of Accra, reminding one of the regrettable period of Ghana's modern history. And Barbara Bonsu, the General's wife, who was behind the media and political attacks, was a staunch member of the ruling party. People called me with stories. They told me Bonsu's ties with the NDC were deep. Apparently deeper than I thought, which is how the premises of the former Ghana National Trading Cooperation (GNTC), a state property, became hers during a previous NDC government.

After the December 1981 coup, the new government built strong relations with Libya. Many Libyans moved to Ghana and enjoyed the goodwill of the government. A group of Libyans ran a duty-free shop at one of the GNTCs and Barbara Bonsu rented a small space there where she sold pastries and drinks. Somewhere down the line, it became public knowledge that the Libyans had purchased the entire premises and given Barbara Bonsu notice to move because they had plans for the strategically located property. This was a blow to her. However, she quickly bounced back. Within a very short time, she went from being an evicted renter of a small space on the property to owner of the entire property. She instead then gave the Libyans notice to vacate the premises. The Libyans protested because they believed they had legally acquired the property. Apparently the matter was discussed at a very high level, and the Libyans were told that Barbara Bonsu, having later put in a bid, was the highest bidder, hence she was the owner of the property.

Those premises are the base of the infamous Media Mafia. I wonder why Barbara Bonsu's investigative journalist and other friends in the media have not enquired into this contentious way of acquiring state property. I wonder why her friends in the media have not written about that.

I called Anna Bossman, the Acting Chairperson of the Ghana Commission for Human Rights and Administrative Justice, to inform her about the letter from the Foreign Ministry terminating African Perspectives' headquarters agreement with immediate effect. She had the mandate to safeguard human rights and investigate alleged human rights abuses. The Commission serves as an ombudsman receiving complaints against public institutions. She asked if I had the mobile number of the officer who had written the letter, Macarious, and I gave it to her. She immediately called him to enquire why the agreement had been terminated. After they talked, Anna called me back to tell me that she had the impression that it was because of the brothel accusations in the media.

Later, Macarious gave an interview in the media claiming that our headquarters agreement had been fraudulently procured. Why would he lie so blatantly? I was puzzled. Macarious seemed to be colluding with the media men I had in court and was probably enjoying the attention.

By comparison with other countries in Africa, Ghana is not so ethnically divided. Yet I wondered if Macarious' conduct had something to do with the common ethnicity of the lead perpetrator of the media assaults, the new Foreign Minister, and Macarious himself. How come the powers that be did not ask me about the brothel allegations? Had they known beforehand that I would be brought into disrepute? What about the subsequent media accusations about fraudulent procurement of a headquarters agreement? Was it part of the plan?

I also informed my lawyer, Godwin, about what appeared to be an urgent termination of our headquarters agreement. He called Macarious to find out about the abrupt termination of the agreement. Macarious told him that Ghana was a sovereign state and free to terminate the agreement. Who said it wasn't? But even a sovereign state could not terminate an agreement without following due process, unless of course there were urgent grounds.

In fact, the government of Ghana had concluded a headquarters agreement with our organisation to enable it to carry out its work freely, and to grant immunities for official duties performed on behalf of the organisation. Even so, it had not been our organisation's idea to conclude such an agreement with the government. The call to the government of Ghana to do so came from a high-level international justice figure who had known our organisation and its work over the years.

In 2003, African Perspectives convened the first major conference to introduce the newly established International Criminal Court to the human rights and justice sectors in Africa. The meeting was held in Accra, where African Perspectives was in the process of establishing its headquarters. It was attended by judges and other high-level officials from the ICC and other international courts and tribunals, civil societies from across Africa, international and intergovernmental organisations, and government officials, among others. At the close of the conference, the international justice official called on Ghana's Minister for

Foreign Affairs, Nana Akufo-Addo, who was officiating at the conference, to conclude a headquarters agreement with African Perspectives. Foreign Minister Akufo-Addo heeded the call, resulting in the headquarters agreement between African Perspectives and the government of Ghana. When Eric Odoi Anim, of the Ministry of Foreign Affairs, invited our organisation to come to the Foreign Ministry to sign the agreement, I asked Ghana Supreme Court Justice Sophia Akuffo, who had recently been elected to the African Court on Human and Peoples' Rights, to witness the agreement for African Perspectives, which she did.

At the time of the media accusations against me, Nana Akufo-Addo had lost his bid for the presidency and was now in opposition. Still, it would have helped if he or any of the other officials who knew about the agreement, and particularly those who had been involved in negotiating it, had come forward to confirm that the agreement had been concluded with their knowledge and involvement. It would have been the right and sincere thing to do, but they stayed mum and allowed the public to falsely believe that I had fraudulently procured a headquarters agreement.

For her part, Justice Sophia Akuffo asked me to write to the new Minister for Foreign Affairs, Alhaji Muhammad Mumuni. She said she'd follow up with him afterwards to tell him she had signed the agreement as a witness for African Perspectives.

But I was not in a position to have direct contact with the new Foreign Minister, who appeared to have been colluding with the media men I had in court for libel and slander following the brothel allegations. I believed that

Mumuni was acting in bad faith. If he was really concerned that I or African Perspectives had fraudulently procured a headquarters agreement, he should have started investigations, instead of the media allegations he and the media men resorted to. Rather, African Perspectives issued a press statement stating how the headquarters agreement had come about and who had been involved in its negotiation and signing.

Furthermore, Mumuni was a controversial figure who had been accused of corruption by a group called Alliances for Accountable Governance. 'There's a terrible commission of enquiry report against him,' a friendly lawyer and member of the ruling NDC party told me. I suspected that a person like Mumuni would be susceptible to the manipulations of the media men I was about to expose in a court of law. Mumuni was apparently a friend of Kweku Baako, Anas' editor-in-chief and co-defendant in the lawsuit. I am told that in an earlier interview Baako was asked about the corruption allegations against Mumuni. His answer was quite revealing: Alhaji Mumuni was his friend and therefore he would not speak against him. This goes to show that Baako is not an independent journalist but one who would cover for his friends, just as he was covering for Barbara Bonsu's lawlessness as well as his and Anas' crimes and instead attacking me.

Shortly after my family and I left Ghana, my lawyer Godwin told me he'd received a call from Nana Oye Bampoe Addo, a renowned human rights and gender advocate and a supporter of the ruling party. She told him she wanted to hold a press conference on our headquarters agreement.

Godwin said Nana Oye was genuine in her offer to help. That did not surprise me, because we had always got along and appreciated each other. She had been baffled when I was libelled in a politicised manner, and had said to me, 'But why you?' Indeed, why me? I was not a politician nor was I political. In the end, however, for some reason the press conference did not take place. Something tells me that Nana Oye was not in a position to go against certain members of the ruling government or persons associated with them. She would later be given the well-deserved position of Minister for Gender and Social Protection in the administration of President John Mahama.

I got another call from Anna Bossman. She had received an unexpected call from a woman who introduced herself as Barbara Bonsu's friend. The woman knew about Anna's conversation with Macarious. Anna had asked how. 'You know, this is Ghana,' the woman had said. She asked Anna to give me a message from Barbara Bonsu. The General's wife said that if I paid her, she would put a stop to everything. Again, we did not owe her anything; it was all part of her bullying. She had not been happy when African Perspectives vacated her premises, even though we gave her the required notice, and had tried to retaliate by threatening to evict Working Girl. These were of course two separate entities, with me being associated with both. And in any case, it was up to the High Court to decide. Yet Bonsu had the audacity to send her message through the Acting Chairperson of the Ghana Commission for Human Rights and Administrative Justice. The General's wife was effectively taking credit for the serial and brutal media assaults against me and for the termination of the headquarters agreement. However, as far as I was concerned, the case was in court, and I believed that both the law and the truth were on our side. I am after all a human rights lawyer, and so would practise what I preached.

I did not realise then that General Bonsu was about to become special adviser to President Mills. General Bonsu had held a key military position in the previous NPP government. The NDC and the NPP are the main and opposing political parties in Ghana. I could not have imagined that having held a sensitive position during Kufuor's first term, the General would now turn around and serve as special adviser to the president of the main rival party. But then again, General Bonsu appeared to have left his position with the previous government on a sour note.

Barbara Bonsu had once lamented to me about how they had found out that the General was being removed from his position after President Kufuor was re-elected to serve a second term. They had learned about the General's removal from office the same time the rest of the country did: through the airwaves. Somehow, Barbara Bonsu had thought he would be appointed ambassador to some country, but that was not to be. So perhaps there was no loyalty lost between the General and the previous government. As it happened, I used to be friendly with Barbara Bonsu before she got married to the General and before African Perspectives rented part of her premises – in fact, before we moved to Accra. Klaas-Jan and I were introduced to Barbara Bonsu's joint by family when we went to Accra for holidays, and we became regular customers, eventually making the fateful decision to rent from her. But as it turned out, the only thing we had in common was that we were both Ghanaian.

I now appreciate an earlier piece of advice I received from a Dutch friend long before we moved to Ghana. I told Linda, who happens to be a psychiatrist, about an encounter I'd had with a woman I used to be friendly with.

'Next time you meet someone, take three minutes to study them,' Linda said, believing that situation could have been avoided if only I had been on my guard. I was raised not to be critical of people with different value systems to mine, so I was rather surprised by Linda's advice.

'But isn't that judgemental?' I asked her.

'Dutch people do not like hassles and so we take our three minutes,' she simply said.

I mentioned Linda's advice to Klaas-Jan, and how I thought it was judgemental.

'You mean you have not been doing that?' He told me that even as a student, when he went to a party he could just look around and determine who he'd get along with and would not give the others his time. But he was also of the view that my non-judgemental approach to people was not only a weakness but also a strength. In the case of my encounter with Barbara Bonsu, it proved to be a major failing. These days I take my three minutes.

It was early evening in the Netherlands and our travel agent there was closed. Klaas-Jan called his brother Harold to tell him what was going on and that we had to flee. He said his brother did not say a word and was only concerned with arranging four tickets quickly. I also told Godwin, my lawyer, that we were making arrangements to leave. Our girls were watching a Disney film when we told them we had to go. They were only seven at the time and didn't understand. In particular, they weren't thrilled that they suddenly had to leave without saying goodbye to their friends.

We had the driver take us to the airport. Kaakra was very upset that she had not been allowed to pack her toys and cried on the way there. Once we got to the airport, the driver put our luggage onto a trolley, but in his rush to get inside, he accidently hit Kaakra's ankle with the trolley. She started bleeding and cried so loudly. With Klaas-Jan carrying her, we went inside to the KLM counter. We were told the counter was closed and that we had to return the next day. Then the KLM director, a Roosevelt parent, appeared. He asked that they check us in.

When we got to immigration, I was asked to present my dual nationality card and those of my daughters. I told them we didn't have dual nationality cards. I had tried many times to get the cards in Ghana, but each time I was told that the Netherlands does not recognise dual nationality and they wondered how my daughters and I had got both Ghanaian and Dutch passports. I told them there are exceptions, and that we fell within them. The immigration officer said we could not leave the country without dual nationality cards. Klaas-Jan told the officer he could not stop us from leaving and that it would be a violation of international law. The officer insisted he could.

So, I separated my Ghanaian passport from my Dutch passport, and Panyin and Kaakra's Ghanaian passports from their Dutch and American passports, and held them out to the officer.

'Here, take them,' I said. 'Take our Ghanaian passports.' The officer froze, not knowing what to say.

'Don't do it Ewurabena,' Klaas-Jan said.

We walked away with our Ghanaian passports. When we got to the final check, a smiling officer took one look at Panyin and Kaakra and said, 'Hello, Obama girls.'

Finally, we boarded the flight. My telephone had been ringing nonstop. There were so many missed calls from my mother and my brother Kobi. I told them we had just boarded the flight.

'Go well, my daughter,' Mum said. 'God will be the final arbiter.'

Another call came in. It was from Godwin. He was in front of our house and said he had some documents he wanted me to sign before I left. He was my counsel, fighting for me. I now appreciated the true meaning of 'counsel'.

I told him, 'We're on the KLM flight; the doors have been shut; the plane is taxiing. We are now officially on Dutch territory.' He started to laugh. I would not advise that anyone try that line. We were very much still on Ghanaian soil.

Godwin would later tell me how sad he had been that I felt compelled to leave. He was certain it was Klaas-Jan who wanted to go. But in fact, it had been my idea. At the time, Klaas-Jan just thought it was a situation that had got out of hand. In our part of the world, too many situations do get out of hand, with dire consequences. Having grown up in coup-prone Ghana, and as a human rights lawyer, I appreciate that rights are fragile, and I was not about to tempt fate. Klaas-Jan would quickly realise that leaving was the only sane decision in the face of such barbarism and danger.

I asked Godwin to let it be known that I had fled the country with my family, and that I would nonetheless continue with the lawsuit. He told me he wouldn't because the defendants would deliberately give it a different meaning. They would announce my departure on the cover of their tabloid newspaper with a bold headline: 'SHE HAS FLED!'

I have never been happier and more relieved to arrive at Schiphol Airport. We took the train to Maastricht. Klaas-Jan's parents and brothers called very early in the morning to find out if we'd arrived, as did my own Mum. She had been so grateful to Harold for having quietly arranged our tickets.

I don't recall much of our arrival in Maastricht, except that I woke up not knowing where we were. All four of us were sleeping in one room, with Panyin and Kaakra on separate mattresses on the floor. I saw my Dad there too. He was wearing one of his African print shirts, the ones he wore to welcome his African American tourists at the international airport in Accra. He had a big smile on his face. He looked strong and fit. His skin was tight, as if he'd had a million oxygen facials. Looking cheerful, Dad told me he was off to the United States.

5

IN MY FATHER'S HOUSE

I AM NOT A STRANGER TO THE NETHERLANDS. However, moving back in a hurry, under stressful circumstances, meant that I had sought refuge there. I was a refugee with a Dutch passport. I went to the police station to file a report about what had happened to me in Ghana.

Since we were now back in Klaas-Jan's country, I was glad that Panyin and Kaakra got a lot of attention from their paternal grandparents and their Aunt Saskia, Klaas-Jan's younger brother's wife, who had two young sons our girls loved to visit and play with. Panyin and Kaakra quickly made friends when they started school six weeks later.

As for Klaas-Jan, he was just happy to be out of Ghana. Although he'd previously loved to visit, he'd seen a different side of Ghana when we moved there – from the land title issues of the community where we'd purchased a home and lived, to the international school with its problematic subculture to the unregulated legal sector. Dad's passing and funeral was another eye-opener. Klaas-Jan would often ask me, 'Is there solidarity in Ghana, or are people only interested in what they can get?' And when he thought he'd seen it all, I was so savagely libelled and slandered, without recourse. To deal with his frustrations, he started writing a thriller based on his experiences and observations in Ghana. In the plot, as the true stories behind the various issues unfold, the protagonist stages his own death and flees the country. When the coffin is opened, the mourners find only bricks in it. But in the end, Klaas-Jan could not finish his novella; it was too painful. It brought back negative emotions about events he did not wish to relive. However, he was reminded of those painful experiences when he read the manuscript of this book, and he cried.

I called the African Perspectives office in Accra to let them know that I had left Ghana until further notice. It was quite sad. The staff members from other countries moved on after their contracts expired. As part of his threats and harassment, Anas sent a video he'd done on another one of his cases to our offices in Accra, while failing to tender his 'evidence' in the spa case into court for quite some time. The Ghanaian staff stayed on until the board decided to freeze the offices in Ghana almost three years later and they found other positions. Prior to their departure, I received a moving letter from them which ended with: 'Long live African Perspectives, and long live Ms Ewurabena.'

Seba had regular contact with the therapists at Working Girl. They were paid the first months after the seizure of the spa and remained hopeful that the spa would soon reopen.

The day after we left Ghana, the front page of a now-defunct tabloid newspaper that rented its premises from Kweku Baako, Anas' editor-in-chief and co-defendant, read: 'O la la, guess who's been stripped of her privileges and immunities?' Due to my suit and application for an injunction against the defendant, Baako could not have written about me without being in contempt of court, so instead his tenant and newspaper colleague wrote about me. This was contemptible. I learned that people in the media repeatedly called out my name on the airwaves, demanding that I return the CD licence plates. Hosts of radio chat shows – friends of Barbara Bonsu, Baako and Anas – through their platforms on the airwaves called on the authorities to deal with the matter. The media threats and harassment intensified. It was barbaric.

Ghanaians and non-Ghanaians who knew me and had read the articles on the internet reached out. A Ghanaian friend in Minnesota wrote, 'I am sure you are truly disgusted by what's happening in Ghana.' A Ghanaian in Germany reached out through a mutual friend to say how sorry she was about the way I'd been treated in Ghana. Another Ghanaian who had relocated to Ghana from the United States and was wondering if he had made the right decision in moving sent an e-mail to say that he was ashamed to be a Ghanaian. A Nigerian scholar in South Africa I knew had also read the article: 'It's irrelevant whether we believe the stories or not. The stories are out there. You've got to fight them,' he said. Kitty, a London-based acquaintance who also owned a house in the community we lived in, reached out later: 'Ewurabena, I couldn't believe my eyes when I read what had been written about you. Those people were out to destroy you.' 'Is Ghana the Wild Wild West?' wrote a friend in London. A US-based Kenyan professor said to me when he heard the story: 'And so underneath the semblance of democracy, there's an underworld in Ghana.' 'Ghana is the untold story,' said a journalist who previously worked at an Africa station of a major media house. These were the reactions of well-meaning people who knew me. They were the sentiments of critical thinkers. But what about the masses who did not know me? What about the institutions and individuals African Perspectives and I would seek support from and explore cooperation with in the near future? Who would want to engage with a brothel runner and a fraudster?

I have no idea how many media outlets carried the stories. A lady I'd got to know through the community where we'd purchased a home called my Dutch mobile. She said one of the radio stations had reported that I'd left the country. She was so relieved that she crossed herself. She said she was calling to get confirmation that I had indeed left. She told me that Paolo was a staunch supporter of the ruling NDC party and begged me not to return to Ghana until they were out of office.

Seba told me she'd received a call from a sympathetic journalist who used to frequent the wellness centre. He told her the media assaults were personal. Indeed, they were, as I used to be friendly with Barbara Bonsu.

There was also a deeper personal dimension. I have reason to believe that our half-cousins once removed colluded with Barbara Bonsu and her media men. Those cousins had not had their way with us on Dad's funeral arrangements about a year earlier. They'd taken this very personally.

When my Dad passed, the eldest of the nine siblings, Sana, had tried to dictate how Dad's funeral should be organised. Aunt Sana's mother, Great Aunt Hatchet, and Dad's mother, Grandma Ewurabena – after whom I'm named – were half-sisters: they had the same father, Nana Kuni. But their mothers, Kyeewa and Nana Yaa, were rivals. According to family stories, there had been no peace in Nana

Kuni and Nana Yaa's household after Kyeewa was brought into their home. However, that was in the past.

Aunt Sana's father, Papa Hatchet, was a trader who migrated from Syria in the 1930s with some of his compatriots. They were on their way to seek greener pastures in the US and thought they had arrived at their destination when the vessel docked at Takoradi Harbour. Papa Hatchet settled in Dunkwa-on-Offin, a town in the central region of Ghana. He was going steady with Kyeewa's admired elder daughter and then, to the surprise of many, he instead got married to Kyeewa's much younger daughter. Great Aunt Hatchet was a child bride, but perhaps at the time child marriage was not frowned upon. She left her Methodist faith to join his Catholic religion and they had eleven children together, while Papa Hatchet had three other children, two of them by his first wife. Aunt Sana was the new couple's eldest child. She later became a retailer of medicines. She lived with her husband in the town of Elmina, developed around the *Castelo da Mina*, built by the Portuguese in 1482. It was the first trading post on the Gulf of Guinea, and the oldest European building in sub-Saharan Africa. After an earlier unsuccessful attempt to seize the castle in 1596, it was taken over by the Dutch in 1637, and then by the British in 1872. Due to this early exposure to and socialising with European settlers, the people of this small town were deemed cultured.

Born of a Ghanaian mother and a Syrian father, Aunt Sana was of mixed race. Superficially she could pass for a privileged local whose male ancestors originated from Portugal, the Netherlands, or the United Kingdom.

However, Aunt Sana was not from Elmina and was not considered as such. This must have bothered her because she liked to rub shoulders. Moreover, while they were growing up in Dunkwa, her father's compatriots looked down on her mother for being black and illiterate. They wouldn't even shake her hand; they would barely touch her fingertips.

She called many times after Dad passed. On one occasion, she asked about the tributes for Dad. She wanted to know who from their family should contribute to the tributes: her mother or herself?

'Your mother,' I said. Her mother made it a point to visit Dad when he was ill. She was also their matriarch, so it made sense for the tribute to be in her name.

'Very well, we'll write it for her'. She would later send a nice tribute in her mother's name.

On another occasion, she informed me: 'Uncle Ishmael says he'll not announce your father's passing unless an emissary is sent with the required schnapps, to formally inform him that your father has passed, and so I have bought schnapps and sent them to him.' I wondered whether she wanted me to pay for the schnapps, and also why she was telling me this, and not my mother. I also thought her remarks were quite insensitive. Is this what you say to someone who had just lost her father? I had heard stories of how extended family members of the deceased had the prerogative to torment the widow and children. I didn't think she would or could. She spoke warmly of my father, and she was not from his matrilineal line in our matrilineal culture. It was getting awkward having regular conversations with her on such an intimate matter on a painful occasion. I personally did not know her that well. I'd see her at the occasional family gathering and we'd exchange pleasantries. I knew her younger siblings in Accra better and had regular interactions with them. But I guess since Sana was the eldest, she felt it was up to her to be having those interactions after Dad's passing.

I tried to gather my composure. 'Who is Uncle Ishmael?' I asked.

'He's your father's uncle.'

I could not imagine that any of Dad's uncles would say such a thing. It would be their duty and honour to play their rightful role for Dad's funeral. None of them would send such a message. Besides, as far as I knew, the youngest of Dad's uncles, whom we knew well, was his only surviving uncle. Uncle Wonderful was his nickname, befitting of his terrific personality. He was not much older than Dad. He had thought Dad was his brother because they grew up together, both of them having been raised by Dad's grandmother, Nana Yaa. Sadly, Grandma Ewurabena had died when Dad and his sisters were all very young. Nana Yaa was his maternal figure, yet he often felt his mother's presence. When Nana Yaa also died, the Hatchets took Dad and his two sisters in, until their father came for them. Great Aunt Hatchet and her kindly Syrian husband had resisted the children being taken away by their father. But this was a family decision. Great Aunt Hatchet was only a paternal aunt, and therefore had no claim to the children. Dad and his sisters went to live with their father. Dad continued to be sustained by the loving spirits of his mother and grandmother. When he grew older, he got close to his maternal uncles who provided guidance and support. In recognition of this, Dad named his youngest child after his late uncle Aboagye.

All in all, Dad did well for himself. On his passing, Jake Henderson Jnr, former President of Henderson Travel and Tours in Atlanta, wrote this tribute:

'I am saddened to hear of Joseph's passing. In many ways I considered him and Elizabeth my uncle and aunt. As a young man when I first visited Ghana, I stayed at the old Ambassador Hotel. At the time, Black Beauty was the only tour operator in Accra ... Joseph picked me up and took me home with him to eat and meet his family. This was the beginning of a tradition ... Our families were not just business partners but true friends. Together they began an activity that perhaps has introduced more African Americans to Ghana or Africa than anyone in history. It is a remarkable achievement for a humble man who always stood tall in both dignity and honor. Although he will be missed, we here will continue to thank God for his existence.'

We had regular meetings in my parents' house to discuss the arrangements for Dad's funeral. Dad's sisters participated in those meetings, and the decision had already been taken that Dad's cousin, Nana Adabo, who had a chieftaincy title in Dad's maternal ancestral home, would take the lead in announcing the funeral. This would be followed by Uncle Wonderful, the various family branches, and indeed the Hatchet family. I told Aunt Sana what had been decided: the Hatchets would be among the announcers of Dad's passing. But that was not enough for her.

'No, no. Uncle Ishmael is the head of the family. He must announce your father's passing and not the chief,' she demanded.

I was confused. I wondered how I'd never heard of this person who Aunt Sana claimed had the authority to announce my father's passing. I had been very close to my father and had learned so much about his childhood in my many conversations with him. As children, we visited Dad's maternal hometown during the Easter breaks, and would also visit his ancestral village. He spoke a lot about his grandmother and his dreams about his mother. He also spoke about his aunts and uncles, including Great Aunt Hatchet and her kind foreign husband, but he never mentioned Uncle Ishmael.

'Is Uncle Ishmael Dad's uncle who lived in the Northern Region?' I asked Aunt Sana. Perhaps that's why I did not remember him.

'Yes,' she replied.

'Okay. He attended our wedding. I remember speaking to him. I'd mistaken him for one of Dad's other uncles because they all looked so much alike. Why did I think Uncle Ishmael died some years back?'

'Actually, Uncle Ishmael is not the uncle who lived in the Northern Region,' she disclosed. Why had she tried to mislead me? She was coming clean because she knew I would soon find out.

'Oh, who's Uncle Ishmael then?' I queried.

'He was brought into the marriage.' In other words, he was not related to Dad by blood. She was speaking in riddles.

'So, he's not actually Dad's uncle,' I said.

'I have just shared a family secret with you. It is a secret locked in a trunk,' she said. Ghanaian folklore is filled with all sorts of tales, and so I was not really concerned about whatever skeleton there might be in the closet.

I told my mother about the conversation with Aunt Sana and her insistence that Uncle Ishmael was the rightful person to announce Dad's passing, not Dad's cousin Nana Adabo.

Mum told me categorically that Nana Adabo was the rightful person to announce Dad's passing and funeral arrangements. She explained to me that Nana Adabo was the younger brother of Dad's late cousin and brother figure, Uncle Badoe. Uncle Badoe was Dad's best man when Dad and Mum got married. Similarly, Grandma Ewurabena, had been the maid of honour to Uncle Badoe's mother, her sister-cousin, Owusua. An only child, Owusua was sent to live with her aunt, Nana Yaa, so that she could be raised with her maternal aunt's – Dad's grandmother's – ten children. Dad's maternal cousins, aunts, uncles and grandmother all descended from one old lady, Dad's great-grandmother, Adjoa Sika. Sika, which means gold, was Adjoa's nickname because she was wealthy.

Uncle Ishmael was not the head of Dad's family, contrary to what Aunt Sana wanted me to believe. He was Aunt Sana's maternal uncle and I assume the patriarch of their maternal family. Sana's grandmother, Kyeewa, had him before moving to Dunkwa to work for Dad's grandparents. Kyeewa had been an owned house-help in the household of Nana Kuni and Nana Yaa, my great-grandparents. The circumstances under which she joined the household were hardly spoken about. It was the big skeleton in the closet. Nana Kuni named the help's son Ishmael, like in the Bible. His own sons he gave the Christian names Isaac, Jacob, Abraham, Joseph, and James, in addition to their Ghanaian names. And as one could do with an owned house-help as they pleased, Nana Kuni ended up having three children with Kyeewa.

Blood relations are important on such occasions, and Uncle Ishmael had no such link with my father. Sana must have known that Mum would have rejected outright her demand to have their uncle announce Dad's funeral. This was why she approached me instead. Mum told me categorically that their Uncle Ishmael was not related to Dad in any way whatsoever.

'How do we solve this?' I asked my mother.

'We'll add him to the uncles and aunts.'

I did not see any reason to report back to Aunt Sana. She called me several times to find out why the obituary was not yet out, and again on the day the obituary was published. 'The announcement is still not in the papers,' Aunt Sana said.

'It is,' I answered.

'I have gone through the obituary section and it's not there.'

'Keep turning the pages of the newspaper – it's there.'

At last, she found the full-page, colour announcement with an imposing and lovely picture of Dad in kente.

'Oh brother,' she said with seeming fondness. 'So how much does such an announcement cost?' I ignored her question. She started to read the announcement. 'Aiye, young lady, you didn't do what I told you to do? You did not let Uncle Ishmael announce your father's passing!'

I was taken aback and took a deep breath. 'He's listed under uncles and aunts,' I said.

'Let your prayers be strong,' she said.

'Excuse me? What do you mean?' I queried.

'If you're not following advice on such an occasion then let your prayers be strong,' she reiterated.

'No one can harm me.'

'Indeed. Your father will protect you from harm,' she said.

I did not want to disturb Mum with what Sana had said. Knowing the narrative of non-peace between Sana's grandmother and Dad's grandmother, Mum would not have taken kindly to her harsh words, especially on such an occasion. Instead, I told my husband.

'She's threatening you because she didn't get her way. What is it with her? She never even visited Dad the entire seven years when he was ill.'

'How do you know?' I asked him.

'Dad told me. We were going through our wedding pictures one day and I saw her in the pictures, and I said to Dad, "This is the woman who turned up to cut our wedding cake with us."'

'And she has not stepped foot in this house since I fell ill,' Dad had said.

I told Mum what I had learned from Klaas-Jan, and she confirmed it. Yet Sana came to Accra often and could have easily stopped by to visit Dad. She would have done so if she considered Dad her kin. At the time of our wedding, I suspected the cake-cutting was a backroom deal she must have cornered Dad into, just like she tried to corner me into making her uncle the announcer of Dad's passing.

In contrast to her silence when he was ill, Sana called Dad often when he was in his prime. She'd lament about how she and her siblings were discriminated against in the town they'd all grown up in. Whenever they stepped on people's toes, they were called slaves because of their grandmother Kyeewa's background. Dad would tell her there were no slaves in modern-day Ghana and so she should disregard those insults.

Sana lobbied for recognition from Nana Yaa's descendants but shunned her own maternal grandmother's – Kyeewa's – lineage altogether. Her desperate pushing for acknowledgement of her mother, uncle and siblings at family events at the expense of Nana Yaa's heirs was legendary. People in Dad's hometown wondered why Sana and her siblings stayed away from their matrilineal line even though they knew their grandmother's hometown. Many believed that they felt superior to their maternal lineage.

Sana's pushiness had no boundaries. Years earlier, she had approached my mother on behalf of one of her younger sisters. Together with her husband, she'd invited Mum and Dad for lunch at a beach resort in Elmina when my parents travelled to the central region.

She said to Mum privately, 'Auntie Lizzy, there's some news.'

'Tell me.' Mum was all ears.

'Kobi and Macy, they'll make the perfect married couple.'

'Good gracious. Is that your news?'

Kobi is my brother and our parents' first son. When Sana persisted, Mum told her she'd never give her blessing to such a union because Dad and Macy's mother were related. Sana insisted that such unions are recognised in their father's Middle Eastern culture. Mum told her that's not our culture. Similarly, when Klaas-Jan's parents and brothers came to Ghana for our wedding, Sana told the brothers she had wives for them too: her youngest sisters. Mina, one of my bridesmaids, an American who lived in the Netherlands, spoke up. She told Sana that one of Klaas-Jan's brothers was there with his girlfriend.

'But they're not married,' Sana said.

Compare: We went with Mum to visit her elderly relative, the Paramount Queen of the Ekumfi State at her home in Accra a few days after our wedding. We also wanted to thank her for her support during the wedding and the baked goods she had sent to my parents' home throughout the period of our wedding. Klaas-Jan's younger brother Harold had been pleasantly surprised to see an iconic picture in the Queen's living room. It was a picture of the young princess and queen-in-waiting riding in a carriage with Queen Elizabeth II of the United Kingdom during her visit to Ghana in 1961.

We were making small talk when the Queen asked Harold: 'Are you married?'

Harold must have thought the Queen also had a wife for him, given Sana's earlier approach. 'Beatrice, will you marry me?' Harold asked the Queen's granddaughter, who he'd already met because she was in the bridal party at our wedding. He was obviously joking.

'No, no,' said the Queen. 'You can't marry her. She's Ewurabena's sister.'

Two of Sana's brothers, Frankie and Jerold, who have since passed on, were such fun. Frankie once took Klaas-Jan out for a local Sunday brunch of *omo tuo* – rice balls served with groundnut soup with fish and spinach – when he first visited Ghana. When he brought Klaas-Jan back home, Klaas-Jan told me how much fun they'd had together, and how he'd been so impressed with Frankie's fluent Arabic.

Arabic? 'Frankie doesn't speak Arabic,' I said.

'Oh yes he does. On our way to the chop bar and back, he saw some of his Middle Eastern friends, and stopped to introduce me to them, and had a chat in Arabic.'

'It's not true. He told a bold-faced lie to you,' I said.

Klaas-Jan would not hear of it. Frankie had charmed him. I said we should ask Dad then. So Klaas-Jan told Dad about the conversations Frankie had had in Arabic on the streets of Accra.

'He doesn't speak Arabic,' Dad said, laughing.

We were also friendly with Sana's youngest sibling, Naima, and her husband, Broomfield. Klaas-Jan had met them at a family function when we moved to Ghana and had got along with Broomfield. They talked a lot about his painting aspirations. Naima and Broomfield soon became regular visitors at our home, sleeping overnight with their children when the electricity in their neighbourhood went off and they could not use their air conditioner because they did not have a generator. Naima's other older sister lived on the way to our house, but she'd still stay in our home, not at her sister's. I'd hear comments from family members that we were being too free with them. Broomfield wanted Klaas-Jan to introduce him to galleries in the Netherlands to promote his works, so Klaas-Jan wrote a letter of invitation for him to obtain a visa to visit the Netherlands. Broomfield visited while I was in Accra with the girls when school was in session. Klaas-Jan took him to galleries in Maastricht, Amsterdam and other cities in the Netherlands. His visit coincided with the yearly Maastricht Fine Arts Fair exhibition, so they went there too. When Broomfield returned to Accra, he told Naima that in Maastricht puppies wore jewellery.

Sana pulled me aside during Dad's funeral. She wanted me to know that Uncle Ishmael had sent a delegation to represent him and introduced me to his daughter. I had the impression Sana was trying to tell me that even though her Uncle Ishmael was not allowed to be the lead announcer of Dad's passing, he had nonetheless sent a representative. However, about a thousand people attended Dad's funeral and none of them had claimed any rights to be the lead announcer of his passing. Sana also handed me an envelope: their contribution to the funeral. I accepted the envelope and thanked her. I wondered why she was giving it to me and not my mother. Other family members who had made donations had done so prior to the funeral and they had handed them to my mother.

The day after we laid Dad to rest, I got a call from Naima and Broomfield. Sana had apparently thought she should have been asked to read Dad's biography. Broomfield told me that if Dad had left funeral instructions, his funeral would have been done differently. He'd never had a conversation with my father, so how would he know? That level of insensitivity was shocking. I had been too free with them and had not appreciated the nuanced and delicate nature of such family relations. Klaas-Jan told me they were just jealous, and that Dad would have loved his funeral. He said Dad would also have loved the fact that some jealous people were discussing it. My husband understood Ghana too well for his own good.

I had not even mentioned my own displeasures with them throughout the funeral preparations. Naima and her other older sister, Josie, had tried to cash in on the funeral. Naima had brought vendors to pitch various things they claimed we would need for the funeral. It turned out their rates were almost double the market price because Naima's commission had been incorporated in the quotes. Josie, a seamstress, kept telling me to come and have my measurements taken so she could make my clothes for the funeral before she got too busy with her Christmas orders. I was surprised at the high costs, but I had already committed myself. I had also ordered two pieces of clothing for a relative attending from North America and paid for hers too when Josie sent me the bill. It turned out the relative had already paid Josie for the cost of her clothes.

After Naima and Broomfield's insensitive remarks about Dad's funeral, I had their envelope with their donation returned. They had it sent back – together with the money for the relative's clothing that had already been paid for – and called me to enquire why I had returned their donation. I didn't go into much detail. Again, Sana threatened me: 'You're lucky we've chosen to resolve it in this way'.

Sadly, Frankie passed on four months after Dad. I found out after Frankie's funeral that Sana had made another rather odd request before the funeral. She'd asked my mother if they could borrow the kente cloth that was used to cover Dad's casket at his funeral service. Mum had agreed to their request and Dad's sister had taken the kente cloth to Sana, which they used to cover Frankie's casket.

'But why the specific kente cloth that had been used for Dad's funeral service?' I asked my mother.

'They probably required a high-quality kente cloth,' she said.

'I am quite sure someone in their family has a nice kente cloth, and if not, they could have bought a nice one, or asked someone else,' I replied. This was not about Frankie. It was about Sana and her other siblings, who by now we suspected were not well-meaning.

When family members in my father's hometown heard that Sana had borrowed Dad's kente cloth, the same one that was used to cover Dad's casket, it did not sit well with them at all.

'You should not have taken it back when they returned it. You should have let them have it,' said a relative.

Frankie was kind-hearted, and Dad had been very fond of him. However, many wondered what Sana and her siblings' real motives were, especially in light of the fallout after Dad's funeral.

The media attacks occurred about a year after Dad's funeral, one week prior to the commemoration of the first anniversary of his passing. Sana and her siblings had not been invited. Sana's younger siblings had an on-off friendship with

Barbara Bonsu. It seemed that as our dispute with Barbara Bonsu intensified, so too did her friendship with the Hatchet siblings. On a number of occasions, Seba saw Barbara Bonsu driving towards Josie's house even though Josie claimed after the media attacks that she was not on friendly terms with Bonsu. In a way, the media assaults were a consequence of Dad's passing.

Mrs Bonsu was eventually convicted of contempt of court for illegally seizing Working Girl and was ordered to return the premises of Working Girl and its belongings. Intriguingly, some hours after Barbara Bonsu was convicted by an Accra High Court, Naima was spotted sitting with Barbara Bonsu and a group of people at Bonsu's joint, presumably consoling her and regrouping. Perhaps Anas and his editor-in-chief Kweku Baako were there too. The conviction and order to return the premises to the spa was proof that Anas and Baako had lied that the spa was subtly operating a brothel and had been closed down by the Ghanaian authorities. It sent a clear message that their story was false. It was a deceit that the Hatchet siblings had contributed to. Naima was seen at Bonsu's joint on the day of her conviction by Surajee, our caretaker, who had been enlisted by Seba to go to Working Girl to help ensure that the court order was being complied with. He knew Naima and her husband because they used to be regular visitors at our home. He was surprised to see her but politely greeted her.

'This is plain jealousy,' Surajee said of the Hatchets' behaviour after he told Seba what he'd seen. Interestingly,

Naima had never been seen at Bonsu's joint the entire time that Working Girl operated from the premises.

We would later receive reliable information that Sana and her siblings had played a behind-the-scenes role in the media attacks against me through their renewed friendship with Barbara Bonsu. Amele, who had been married to one of the Hatchet brothers, told a relative about the Hatchets' role in the media attacks. She said that Naima would bring information from Mrs Bonsu's joint and then Sana would have the final say on how they would use the information against me.

Amele herself had encountered their wrath when she expected financial help from the Hatchets after her husband died. She had not been able to work the entire time he was ill because she had to tend to him and their young daughter. They even took it out on their own niece, Amele's seven-year-old girl, who was herself having difficulty dealing with the loss of her father. Naima had included her young niece as one of the flower girls in the wedding of their cousin. Amele's daughter had attended dress fittings and rehearsals with the wedding party, when Naima unceremoniously pulled her out, much to the disappointment and sadness of the young child, who experienced her aunties' viciousness. Amele is reported to have said that she didn't know the Hatchets could be so wicked.

Some of Dad's relatives were not surprised when they learned about the role Sana and her siblings had played in the media attacks. They had also been on the receiving end of the Hatchets' harsh treatments. Some of our cousins complained about how the Hatchet siblings and their mother had interfered with Uncle Wonderful's will and had tried to disinherit some of his children. A will that named his oldest living nephew, Uncle Reverend, as executor distributed his estate to all his children. Then a second will emerged. Two things in the second will stood out. Firstly, it had been witnessed and signed by a worker of Great Aunt Hatchet, suggesting to many that the Hatchets, or at least their mother, might have had a hand in its preparation. Secondly, the will disinherited Uncle Wonderful's first wife and her children – with whom, incidentally, the Hatchets were not on speaking terms. Rather, the will bequeathed Uncle Wonderful's entire estate to his second wife and her children, who were close to the Hatchets. I didn't realise he had a second wife until I was an adult. As children, when we visited Dad's hometown we stayed with Uncle Wonderful and his family. I do not believe that Uncle Wonderful would disinherit his first wife and their children.

Sana hired a lawyer for the second wife to challenge the will. This action was the Hatchets' way of harassing the older wife, her children, and Uncle Reverend, with whom the Hatchets had fallen out when another one of Dad's uncles died five years earlier. One set of cousins in Accra were so furious about this injustice that they made copies of both wills and circulated them among the family members, asking us to judge for ourselves which of the wills was valid. Even though Uncle Wonderful's wives did not get along, his children did, and here were the Hatchets playing divide and rule against siblings.

Poor Uncle Reverend was the defendant in the lawsuit. He travelled regularly from Accra to Cape Coast where the case was being heard. Uncle Wonderful's oldest daughter also travelled often from Dunkwa to Cape Coast to represent their mother and her children. Three years later, the suit was abandoned, and the wives and children held on to the properties they were in possession of at the time of Uncle Wonderful's passing, just as had been stipulated in the will that named Uncle Reverend as executor.

When Great Aunt Hatchet passed, Sana called Uncle Reverend on several occasions. The first call was to inform him of her mother's passing. In subsequent calls she reminisced about her mother's life and also spoke about the funeral arrangements. She tried to cosy up to him as if she and her siblings had never falsely accused him in a court of law. In their mother's obituary, Uncle Reverend was listed first amongst the nephews and nieces. They also listed our father's family name, though as Mum cynically said, 'It's not us, it's Dad's sisters.' Sana reached out to my older brother Kobi to tell our family that their mother had passed. It was a formality; we already knew.

No one from Dad's nuclear family attended the funeral. Too much had happened, and while much could have been forgiven, their role in the media assaults involving lies that I was running a brothel was the last straw. Instead of calling her children to order, Great Aunt Hatchet, who had had a warm relationship with Dad, had rather spread the fabrications to relatives. One of those relatives told me she was praying for me. She asked me to fast and not eat or drink till midday, and if possible, not to eat till six PM. She told me she did not even know how to articulate what Great Aunt Hatchet had said. It was not up to us to forgive or not forgive. That was a matter between the perpetrators and their God.

Uncle Wonderful's older children, who the Hatchets had tried to disinherit, also did not attend the funeral. However, one of their siblings in North America, after seeking permission from her older siblings, called Sana to send her condolences to the Hatchet siblings.

Uncle Reverend also did not attend Great Aunt Hatchet's funeral, not even after the various calls from Sana. 'What if I attend the funeral and they point me out as the nephew who forged the will,' Uncle Reverend said wryly.

Many in Dad's family have shown negative feelings about their encounters with the Hatchets. An elderly relative told me, after the fallout with the Hatchets, 'People know about the things their grandmother Kyeewa did when she came to serve in our family after she and her infant son were banished from their own hometown. In the same way, what they did to you by collaborating with the media men will be known for years to come,' she said.

My elderly family members told me stories, stories that were never told in our home and stories that would not have been told to me had Sana not insisted that their Uncle Ishmael be the announcer of Dad's funeral arrangements. The stories were eerie. I got to know more when I coordinated a book to honour Dad's memory. The biggest elephant in the conversations I had with my elderly relatives had to do with the Hatchets and their lineage through their grandmother. The Hatchets' grandmother and her son, Uncle Ishmael, were referred to as 'some of the occupants of the house', while Dad's grandparents and their descendants were referred to as 'your father's grandparents, mother, uncles and aunties'.

What was the story with Sana's grandmother, Kyeewa? How did she and her son come into Dad's grandparents' household?

'They were sold off,' an elderly woman said bluntly.

I couldn't believe my ears. Is this what Sana had meant when she referred to 'a family secret locked in a trunk'? It was in fact an open secret, but no one had told me about it. Come to think of it, I vaguely recalled that there were issues with the Hatchets and their heritage. But that didn't matter; they were family. I only wanted to understand Sana's insistence that someone not related to my father should be the lead announcer of Dad's funeral arrangements.

'But why would they do that to a mother with a young child?' I asked the elderly woman who revealed Kyeewa's background to me.

'Her own family had to banish her from her hometown,' she told me. 'Sadly though, their relief was another's misery. Your great-grandfather had three children with Kyeewa, and there was no peace in the household. One calamity after another befell Nana Yaa, your Dad's grandmother, and her older daughters. Like grandmother, like grandchildren. Sana and her siblings took after their grandmother. It's in the blood,' she said.

'But that's not fair. They're not responsible for their grandmother's actions,' I said.

'A child you are,' she said to me.

I was also told a story that, unbeknownst to me, had been told and retold.

The day Dad's grandmother died, her rival, Kyeewa, prepared the festive meal of *eto,* an orange-coloured dish of mashed yam with palm oil and hard-boiled eggs. *Eto* is served on birthdays, when a girl reaches puberty, and on other joyous occasions. Kyeewa ate *eto* the day Dad's grandmother died.

Kyeewa then joined the mourners who had come to pay their last respects to Dad's grandmother, who was lying in state in the large living room. The mourners filed past, as did Kyeewa, wailing the death of her rival. Suddenly, she choked, and threw up. The orange *eto* dish, the egg white, and yellow yolk all came out. The mourners saw what Kyeewa had eaten the day her rival died: the festive meal of *eto.* Kyeewa quickly left the funeral and was not seen for several days.

'How Kyeewa was ashamed,' said the elderly relative. 'Ewurabena, I say, this is not folklore. I saw it with my own eyes.'

6

NKRUMAH WILL TURN

SHORTLY AFTER WE RETREATED TO THE Netherlands, I called Roosevelt School's administration to tell them Panyin and Kaakra would return the following quarter, though we would later change our minds about going back to Ghana when Obama got involved. The Ghanaian lady I spoke to recognised me and expressed sympathy. She said the elementary school principal – the principal who had been working without a visa or work permit – had come to their office to ask them if they'd seen the stories about me on a website read largely by Ghanaians in Ghana, Ghanaians abroad and expatriates. She said the principal was going around the school excitedly asking people if they had read the stories. Together with another Ghanaian staff member, she went to the website to read the stories. They looked at each other in amazement. Her colleague said, 'Look at what these people have done to this strong board member.'

The perpetrators used the Ghana News Agency (GNA) to spread their disparaging stories far and wide. The GNA was founded by Kwame Nkrumah in 1957 when Ghana gained its independence, during the decolonisation struggle in Africa. It was part of Nkrumah's project to ensure that Africans tell their own stories, instead of African stories being told by neo-colonialists, imperialists and others with self-serving motives. Thus, the GNA was established for a noble goal. It is a paradox that the GNA was used to disparage the only Ghanaian on the American school board who was raising issues about unfortunate practices at the school.

One of GNA's foreign correspondents, a friend in London, had been alarmed to receive the article written about me and called immediately.

'I told you,' he said. What was he talking about?

'You told me what?' I asked, quite confused.

'I told you that we should develop a human rights training programme for the African media. This would not have happened if we were training Ghanaian journalists,' he said.

Indeed, we should train and engage the media on human rights and international justice, and we had tried to raise funds for such a comprehensive and long-term training. In the meantime, we organised press conferences for the media to engage with human rights and justice sectors during our workshops. But seriously, did they need me to tell them not to fabricate stories? Must they be told not to make up stories, not to libel and slander? Did they really need to mislead the world into thinking that I was running a brothel? Many believed that it was all so personal, and yet I did not even know the journalists behind the attacks: Anas Aremeyaw Anas and Kweku Baako.

The elementary school principal would later trick Klaas-Jan into signing a form stating that we were temporarily not members of the Roosevelt community when we asked them to reserve a place for Panyin and Kaakra for the next quarter.

She then took the form to the school board to orchestrate my removal from the board. In an e-mail to the school board, Klaas-Jan expressed surprise about how he had been misused to facilitate my removal from the school board, and how he found it all so inappropriate. I was not aware because I had been travelling for work and had limited access to e-mails.

It was Major Holly, the presumed representative of the US ambassador on the school board, who responded to Klaas-Jan's message. The American soldier entitled his group e-mail message with its insulting contents: 'Holly is Shooting'. He told my husband that *he* was inappropriate. How so? Was it because he's married to an African woman – a black woman? Or was it because his wife was falsely accused in the media of running a brothel due to her critical stance on rule of law issues? A stance she also took on the American school board. I found Major Holly's message highly offensive and wrote to the US ambassador to complain. I told him that my husband – incidentally a fine legal scholar – is very appropriate. Ambassador Teitelbaum did not respond. Or perhaps he did, weeks later, through Obama's message to Africa in which he praised Anas Aremeyaw Anas for telling the truth. What was so curious about Obama's endorsement was that Teitelbaum knew about my much-publicised defamation suit against Anas. Interestingly, I later discovered, after making calls and speaking to someone in Washington DC who had had something to do with Obama's speech, that the name and praise of the reporter had not been in the written address when Obama left for Ghana.

Back in the Netherlands, I had an encounter with Shivansh, from the Roosevelt school board, when we put our house in Ghana up for rent. Andre, the person who was interested in renting the house, was an expatriate who had recently arrived in Accra and worked at the same multinational bank as Shivansh. He'd gone to look for a house in the gated community and saw our house. He loved it and the rent was within the price range that his company was prepared to pay. He took pictures and sent them to his wife who was still in South Africa and preparing to join him in Accra. She loved it too. So, Andre sent us his company's standard contract. He wanted the house for three years, but according to company policy they would pay two years upfront. They would keep our caretaker, who would continue to stay in the caretaker's quarters. It was not bad at all, so we signed the contract and sent it back for their signature. The contract was to start at the beginning of the calendar month, but the company had been slow to return the signed contract. Andre asked if he could move in with his family while the process was being finalised. We agreed and they moved in. We were not concerned at all because, after all, the lessee was a major multinational bank. However, weeks went by and we had still not received the contract. I followed up more than once. Andre promised to find out what the hold-up was and get back to us. A couple more weeks went by and there was still no news. Finally, he told me he had traced the contract. It was on the desk of their Chief Financial Officer – Shivansh. I did not have a good feeling about that. Could this explain the delay? What was Shivansh up to? Klaas-Jan calmed me down. This was, after all, a multinational company. What could Shivansh possibly do, given that his colleague had picked a house he clearly loved and had already moved in? Andre came back with information.

'They say I must move,' he told me.

'Really? Why?' I asked him.

He said he did not know, but that he was going to report it to his boss, a lady in their offices in Nigeria. A couple of days later he called to tell me that Shivansh said we could call him.

At the time, Shivansh was still the school board president at Roosevelt. After we left the country, the school refused to refund us the unused tuition we had paid for Panyin and Kaakra's school fees unless we signed an undertaking not to sue the school. Very interesting. We did not sign, and they failed to refund us the tuition. Why would we sue the school if they refunded the unused tuition? What else had they done that would justify our suing them?

'I told you there is more going on in that school,' Klaas-Jan said.

We did not call Shivansh. Instead, I called his general manager, a Ghanaian, and explained to him what had happened. He was quite a pleasant man. He said it might be that their new colleague had chosen a house that was more expensive than the rent allowance the company had allotted him. I assured him that was not the case. I was later informed that they had asked Andre to move to an unoccupied house that belonged to the company where he would not have to pay rent. This time Andre did not resist, for it sounded like a lucrative offer.

I called the company's legal division. The legal adviser was not there, so I spoke to his deputy. She knew about the matter. She said Shivansh had gone to see her to enquire what it would take to cancel the contract. Even he must have realised that although the company had not sent us the executed contract, they had made an offer and we had accepted; their official had already moved into the house, and so there was a contract. The deputy legal adviser told me she had informed Shivansh that they could pay for three months and get out of the contract. She also told me that one of her colleagues had said, 'Ewurabena is one strong lady.'

Klaas-Jan had been particularly disappointed that the Ghanaian leadership at the bank did not take a stance. The CEO was Ghanaian, as was the Head of the Legal Division. He concluded that Shivansh must have brought in some high-net-worth clients, perhaps from Roosevelt. He sent an e-mail to the bank's CEO and the Head of the Legal Division. His e-mail was entitled 'Nkrumah Will Turn'. Dr Kwame Nkrumah was of course the pan-African freedom fighter and the first president of Ghana. Nkrumah famously proclaimed in his independence address that Ghana, our beloved country, was free forever. However, is Nkrumah's Ghana free?

In his e-mail to Shivansh's colleagues, Klaas-Jan wrote that this was a multinational bank in Ghana, with a Ghanaian CEO and a Ghanaian legal counsel, and yet it seemed to endorse the unfair stance of their Chief Financial Officer, who was from another country and an ally of the American ambassador, against a Ghanaian.

My husband is right in his opinion about the lack of solidarity in Ghana. Why else would the citizens of a country so endowed with natural resources like gold, cocoa and oil be so desperately poor? Yet some politicians become instantly rich when they gain political power, and they are admired for it.

Our people are also good at finishing each other off, and I should know that. There's even a term for it: 'pull him or her down', abbreviated to 'PhD'. PhD practices can go very far – from petty jealousy to killings.

I was saddened to hear that PhD practices were common in other African countries too. This may not be an African problem but a problem of lawlessness – barbarism and lawlessness being two sides of the same coin. A Ugandan colleague told me that in his country 'PhD' stands for 'permanent head damage'. A colleague from Togo and Benin provided an analogy from the two neighbouring countries involving big crabs. Due to their size, big crabs are very capable of climbing. Yet when you put several of them together in a bucket and leave it uncovered, they do not climb out of it; instead, they use their strength to pull one another down. As humans, we can, and should, do better than crabs.

Indeed, such behaviour seems to conflict with the so-called African philosophy of existence. African communities have been said to embrace the collective, thereby showing solidarity with one another. In other words, as one scholar puts it: 'I am because we are, and since we are therefore I am.'[1] Thus, living in Africa means 'abandoning the right to

---

[1] John S. Mbiti, *African Religions and Philosophy* (London: Heineman 1969), p. 144.

be an individual, particular, competitive, selfish, aggressive, conquering being in order to be with others, in peace and harmony with the living and the dead, with the natural environment and the spirits that people it or give life to it.'[2] Whatever happened to that African sense of Ubuntu?

For his part, Klaas-Jan uses the metaphor of football, his favourite subject, to drive his point about the lack of solidarity home. He tells me Ghana has excellent football players, but somehow when they come together to play in the national team, they do not do as well as they could because they do not play as a team. They play like individuals. It appears that one of the few times some of my compatriots are able to work as a team is when they conspire to disparage or stage a coup d'état. Kwame Nkrumah stood for solidarity, but that is not how Ghanaians treat their own. That is not how this multinational bank in Ghana, with a Ghanaian CEO and a Ghanaian legal counsel, treated a fellow Ghanaian. Nkrumah will, indeed, turn in his grave.

---

[2] Keba M'Baye and Birame Ndiaye, 'The Organisation of African Unity (OAU)', in Philip Alston, *The International Dimensions of Human Rights* (Westport, Connecticut: Greenwood Press & Paris-Unesco, 1983) p. 589.

7

AMY COOPER MOMENTS

ANOTHER STORY WHICH THE MEDIA MEN TOLD to discredit me further involved the German Development Agency, GTZ as it was called then. They claimed that African Perspectives had only accounted for three thousand and three hundred euros out of a grant of forty thousand euros. That amount was GTZ's contribution to our organisation's pan-African conference to introduce the new African Court on Human and Peoples' Rights to the human rights and justice sectors in Africa. Two other donors contributed to the conference, but GTZ made the largest contribution. We invited participants from many African countries and covered the costs of their travel, accommodation and all meals, and conference costs. The meeting was held in Accra, in cooperation with the Office of the Attorney-General and Ministry of Justice of Ghana, which was to contribute fifty percent of the budget. The meeting attracted high participation from Ghana itself. It was our largest international conference yet in Ghana, with about one hundred and forty participants, including some fifty international attendees. The conference room was so packed that when I left my seat at the high table after the opening ceremony, I could not find an empty seat anywhere else in the room.

We actually did not approach GTZ for funding. It was the Dutch Embassy in Accra that invited GTZ to meet us to discuss our project, given that the funds we had anticipated from the Netherlands had already been depleted and they hoped that other development partners could provide support. Mechthild Runger, the GTZ programme officer, represented GTZ at the meeting and immediately offered to contribute forty thousand euros to our conference after I briefly explained its objectives. They had received the agenda with the impressive list of speakers ahead of the meeting. Still, forty thousand euros after a ten-minute pitch was a record for our African-initiated, African-driven, and African-led organisation. The transfer was equally expeditious, and within a very short time the funds were in our organisation's account. However, I should have known that there would be a catch to such easy and quick money. Shortly after the transfer arrived, I received a call from Mechthild Runger.

'We've transferred the funds,' she announced.

'Yes, we've received them, thank you very much. We were about to write to you to acknowledge receipt,' I said.

'I'd like to know what role we will play,' she said.

I was not quite sure what she meant because a possible role for them had not been mentioned at the meeting, nor in the signed contract. They had simply donated money on the basis of the proposal submitted by African Perspectives.

'Your support will be acknowledged in the conference programme and the narrative report we will issue after the meeting, as well as a forthcoming African Perspectives quarterly journal that we will dedicate to the new African Court.' That would be quite significant publicity they would receive in return for their altruism. 'We will of course provide a financial report on how your funds have been used,' I added.

This was how I was used to working with funders. But our main dealings with traditional funders occurred outside Africa. African Perspectives was founded in the Netherlands because I was living there when I conceived of it. Our first offices were on the premises of Maastricht University, where I had completed my tenure as a visiting research scholar. From what I know of grantor–grantee relationships, at least for an organisation operating from Europe, it would be frowned upon if a development cooperation agency were to pay money in return for favours, as it were.

'We are not donors, we are partners; we must be assigned a role,' Mechthild Runger insisted.

That was interesting. As if an African-initiated and African-led organisation could be true partners with a well-endowed German development agency we had been introduced to less than a week ago. I suppose it could be possible. No one says that a partnership must be between equals.

'What role did you have in mind?' I asked her.

'We'd like our ambassador to speak at the opening, after the African Union Commissioner for Political Affairs.'

Ah. Were they buying a speaking spot at our conference? Quite an expensive spot, I'd say. Maybe we should stop fundraising and instead sell speaking spots at our high-profile conferences.

I did not know how to accommodate that; the opening ceremony was already packed with speakers. Besides, I had another problem: Germany was not the only contributor to this conference. The country office of the United Nations Development Programme had made a modest contribution, as had one other contributor. How could I justify assigning the German ambassador such a prominent role, and not the other contributors?

I mentioned this to a Ghanaian dignitary.

'What do you care? Let the man come and talk; collect your money,' he told me. It sounded very pragmatic. Perhaps this is how they were used to dealing in Ghana.

In the end we found a compromise, or so I thought. The German ambassador would speak at the concluding panel, which also had some high-profile participants. However, the next day, Mechthild Runger called to inform me that her ambassador would not attend the conference after all. Instead, she, as programme officer, would speak at the panel discussion to conclude the conference alongside African dignitaries including a United Nations Assistant Secretary-General and a Justice of the Supreme Court of Ghana.

I was surprised to learn from the Attorney-General's Office that the funds we had received from GTZ had been promised to them. They turned out to be the same funds the Attorney-General would have used as their contribution to the conference. I wondered why GTZ had chosen to divert those funds to our organisation. GTZ only informed the Attorney-General's Office about the diversion when the latter followed up to enquire about the promised grant. Yet GTZ never told us that they were sending the contribution they had promised the Attorney-General's Office to our organisation instead. It was quite complicated and not what

I would have expected from a well-meaning funder. This also meant that the conference was underfunded, as the contribution we had anticipated from the Attorney-General's Office was no longer forthcoming. At least we were used to running our activities on a low budget.

The conference itself was a huge success. GTZ was acknowledged in all the conference documents. We submitted our narrative and financial reports of the conference, which were accepted by all funders except GTZ. In a series of letters to me and copied to some of the dignitaries who attended the conference – Ghana Supreme Court judges, the Attorney-General, my board – they claimed we had only accounted for three thousand seven hundred euros of their grant and demanded that we return the rest. It was remarkable. It takes an entitled person to take such liberties and also make an unreasonable demand like that. Runger knew the power of her whiteness, even in an African country. Who would believe an African recipient over a white donor? In their dealings with Africans, white donors often presumed fraud – although they were unlikely to mind if they got their way. A Dutch friend who works in development cooperation once told me that donors believe they can always nail an African for fraud if they want to. This is because they make the rules and so they can always apply them to suit their purposes. Therefore, like in police brutality cases in Europe and North America, African grantees are several times more likely to be wrongly accused of fraud by white donors than their Caucasian counterparts. As a result, some African NGO executives have been compelled to hire Caucasians to be their focal points with donors.

GTZ did not accept our expenditures, except for some printing costs and one airfare. In a time of e-tickets they insisted on ticket stubs, which only the participant from the International Criminal Tribunal for Rwanda could provide. Since they were so insistent, we invited GTZ to come to our offices, go through the relevant bank statements and compare them with the corresponding invoices, but they declined. We had our auditors perform a conference-specific audit, but GTZ still declined the auditors' report. The forty thousand euro contribution from GTZ was captured in our audited account of that year. Still GTZ insisted that we pay back money that had already been spent on the conference, and for which they had received wide acknowledgement. They sued. We asked the Ministry of Foreign Affairs to mediate because we could not participate in the lawsuit by virtue of our headquarters agreement. They continued with the suit. We invoked our headquarters agreement, and the case was dismissed.

A friendly acquaintance working for the Ghana judicial service told me about another encounter with Runger. Through GTZ, Runger had sued a gentleman they had a good working relationship with over funding issues. My acquaintance also told me that GTZ micromanaged them whenever they gave them a grant. She said Runger would set up a desk at their workshops to collect receipts from participants. That's a new one. I would actually not have minded if GTZ had suggested that as part of their grantmaking. I would have been happy to let them try to collect ticket stubs from conference participants. But they had no such condition or any others beyond normal reporting. It seemed the unwritten condition was that their ambassador speak after the African Union Commissioner for Political Affairs. And since they did not get the front-row seat they thought they were entitled to, they wanted their money back.

Mechthild Runger continued to write disparaging letters to me, copying various dignitaries. I responded, copying those she'd copied. Interestingly, Runger's letters always referred to me as Elizabeth instead of Ewurabena, even after I repeatedly informed her in my replies that my name was Ewurabena, not Elizabeth. After I was libelled, I noticed that some of the articles published about me on the internet likewise referred to me as Elizabeth. Had GTZ shared our correspondence with the media men or their allies? If so, under what circumstances? Why were we not consulted to get our position about the information shared? Incidentally, when I joined the Roosevelt school board, I got to know that the GTZ country director was a parent and member of the Roosevelt community. She was also a supporter of the school superintendent who was being let go, and the superintendent had shared her letter of support for him. When the GTZ issue became part of the news about our headquarters agreement and its termination, I wondered if their country director had had occasion to discuss this within the Roosevelt community too.

My board chair also wrote to GTZ to reiterate our position. Klaas-Jan suggested to me that we lift our headquarters agreement and challenge GTZ in court. What would have been the point of a headquarters agreement then? During the dispute with GTZ, our office in The Hague received a letter from the German Ministry of Foreign Affairs asking how a sum of ten thousand euros they had contributed to one of our activities years ago had been spent. This was clearly triggered by the dispute with GTZ in Accra. We re-sent them the report as well as the audit in which the expenditure was captured, and fortunately they were satisfied.

After my family and I moved back to the Netherlands, I reached out to the GTZ headquarters in Germany and went there for a face-to-face meeting. I told them about how things had escalated with their office in Accra, and how I'd been accused in the media of running a brothel. Given that things had really got out of hand with their office in Ghana and I was now working from our offices in The Hague, I asked them to take over the dispute from their office in Ghana. We still had a small office in Accra, but I was the person they had dealt with on this issue. I also believed it would be much easier for them to bully our organisation in Ghana, where the authorities craved being on their good side, than it would be in Europe – despite racist tendencies. The two men I met with at the GTZ headquarters were quite sympathetic. They said they'd get back to me. I guessed it would be normal for them to consult with their office in Ghana first.

I did not get a response from their headquarters and never heard from their offices in Ghana again. However, in November 2020, during an interaction with the German Embassy in The Hague, the GTZ issue came up. They were wondering how the litigation had ended because while GTZ had informed the German Foreign Ministry when they demanded that their contribution be returned – their way of blacklisting African Perspectives – they had nonetheless failed to inform their Foreign Ministry about the outcome of the litigation. I told the German Embassy in The Hague that we had never heard from GTZ again. I assumed they'd abandoned their dubious lawsuit. The next day they informed me that they had contacted GTZ in Ghana, who said that an Accra court had issued a judgment requiring our organisation to pay GTZ the amount they were demanding. They claimed that at the time of the judgment African Perspectives no longer had an office in Ghana and no representative could be found. That was odd. It was the first time I was hearing about it. African Perspectives had a lawyer on record, and they'd obviously not tried to reach him. Besides, our offices in Ghana had only closed in 2012, three years after I left, and those were the same offices they'd been sending their letters to. Additionally, they knew how to reach me and our offices in The Hague and yet they failed to do so. Furthermore, is it not curious that they had not informed their Foreign Ministry about the outcome of the litigation when they had been quick to tell them when the dispute arose? Sometime earlier, during the defamation, our lawyer told me that GTZ's lawyer had casually informed him that his clients were quite nervous about the case and wanted it finalised as soon as possible. No wonder they did not tell their Foreign Ministry about the questionable outcome of the case.

African Perspectives had been wronged. It was an Amy Cooper moment.

Amy Cooper is a white woman. On the 25th of May 2020, she took her dog for a walk in Central Park in New York City. She saw a black man watching birds in a section of the park called the Ramble. His name was Christian Cooper, but they were not related. The black man asked the white woman to put her dog on the leash, but she refused to. So, he did what many dog owners despise: he beckoned the dog towards him with a dog treat.

'Don't you touch my dog,' she yelled at him. He started recording her, and she told him not to. He continued to record. She told him she'd call the police.

'Please call the cops,' he said with a seriousness and quaver in his voice that suggested that he knew too well that the police and black men are like oil and vinegar. Such a call could cause him harm, even death.

Amy Cooper knew that too. 'I'm going to tell them there's an African American man threatening my life,' she threatened him. She carried out her threat and called the New York Police Department. However, both of them had left by the time the police responded. Christian Cooper's video of the incident went viral.

An Amy Cooper moment occurs when white people misuse the automatic privilege that comes with their whiteness against a black person, or any person of colour, knowing that they will be backed by the powers that be. The white person's word is usually believed over the black person's word, unless the former's racism is caught on camera.

Having lived in Europe and America from a relatively young age, I have had my fair share of Amy Cooper moments. One of my Amy Cooper moments in Europe involved an encounter with a clothing store attendant in Maastricht in 2013, long before the Amy Cooper incident in

Central Park occurred. The store attendant said she'd call the police on me simply because I wanted to exchange a faulty suit. The store attendant knew the power of her whiteness over a black person. She didn't call the police, but I called Klaas-Jan, who arrived in a matter of minutes because his office was just around the corner. He asked the woman why she had threatened to call the police. Her response was that they had not received any complaints about the brand of clothing I was trying to return. Klaas-Jan announced to the other shoppers: 'I wouldn't buy anything from this store if I were you. Their high-priced clothes are of poor quality.' Feeling somewhat empowered, I told the store attendant that I did not want to exchange the suit; I wanted my money back. She obliged.

Amy Cooper would become a prelude to George Floyd, who was killed 'in broad daylight', incidentally on the 25th of May 2020, the same day the Amy Cooper incident occurred. Floyd was handcuffed and in the custody of three policemen, one of them kneeling on Floyd's neck, even when he told them he couldn't breathe. They snuffed the life out of him. The Floyd case reminds me of the 1998 killing of Semira Adamu, a twenty-year-old Nigerian woman who fled her country because of a forced marriage. She died in the custody of Belgian police officers who were deporting her. They placed her face in a pillow on the lap of one of the officers and she suffocated to death. What was surprising was the insistence of Belgian authorities that the officers were trying to calm her down by forcing her face into the pillow. They snuffed the life out of her too.

While the seriousness of Amy Cooper offences cannot be compared with the gravity of so-called international crimes – those crimes that are so grave that they are considered to be crimes against the human race – they nonetheless have certain similarities and can both be classified as offences of international concern. Each of them tends to be systemic, they are excessive, an outrage, and they are unconscionable. You can feel the unimaginable pain of the victim or the offended irrespective of where you live in the world, but perhaps more so if you have something in common with them. The actions of the entitled offender who takes certain liberties because of their race or position in society is an affront to people everywhere.

The murder of George Floyd was of international concern. It was an act of systemic police brutality perpetuated against black people. Floyd's death could have been dismissed as having been caused by a 'medical incident during police interaction', as stated in the report filed by the police, which omitted the police's own role in Floyd's death. Then a video filmed by one brave seventeen-year-old girl appeared. The footage of Floyd's death shocked the conscience of humankind. There was an international outcry. Our daughters joined their white friends in our predominantly white city to protest. I must admit that I was concerned about their participating in a demonstration during the Covid-19 pandemic but was assured that the proper measures were in place, with law enforcement present, and the risks minimal. Upon return, the girls reported that their role had involved chanting in response to the well-known slogan. After they gathered in a park, two of the protestors – a black woman and her white husband – stood before them and shouted:

'BLACK LIVES'

'MAAATTER,' they chanted.

Growing up in Ghana, we learned about the crime of apartheid in far-away South Africa. I read more about apartheid in my literature class. Peter Abrahams' melancholic novel, *Mine Boy,* exposed me to what life was like for blacks in South Africa. There were students from South Africa's neighbouring Namibia in my school. We knew they had come to Ghana because they were discriminated against in their own country simply because of the colour of their skin. They told us their stories. Some of them had lost their parents and other family members because of racism. Some of them never knew their parents as a result of bigotry. Our Ghanaian passports read: 'valid for all countries except South Africa'. There were no plans for me to visit South Africa, yet I felt that apartheid was a crime against me. So, when I became a student of international criminal justice, it was very easy for me to grasp that certain crimes are crimes against the human race.

I would suggest, however, that Amy Cooper moments are strictly speaking not limited to black–white issues. They are above all, matters of dominance. Who has the upper hand? Who will be backed by the powers that be? Who can bulldoze their way through a situation because of who or what they represent? Who can get away with causing harm to others? Barbara Bonsu knew that the militant government with which she had links was in power and her husband the General was in government, and therefore she could do an

Amy Cooper job on me and get away with it. Likewise, the Roosevelt School officials knew that they were backed by the Republican American ambassador, the representative of the United States of America in Ghana. With the US ambassador on their side, they could rely on the diplomatic weight of the United States more generally, and perhaps even the President, Barack Obama himself, during his visit to Ghana. Obama's endorsement of a defendant in a highly publicised and ongoing defamation lawsuit was quite contentious. Personally, I am not sure which is worse: encountering Amy Cooper moments in my native Ghana or having a white person misuse their whiteness against me in Europe and America. Both can have fatal consequences.

Obama's endorsement in and of itself probably did not count as an Amy Cooper moment because Obama himself was the authority whose backing was desired. Unless the endorsement was meant to influence public opinion and the judges of the law courts, in which case it would have been an Amy Cooper moment. Or perhaps Obama's endorsement as such did count as an Amy Cooper moment because he would have been believed because of the esteem in which he was held, in the same way that the police would have believed Amy Cooper because of her whiteness. I have wondered whether Teitelbaum would have put Obama up to making that same endorsement if Anas had accused a white American or European female lawyer and Roosevelt School board member in the media of running a brothel. I very much doubt that he would have.

At the time of Obama's pronouncements, he was the leader of the Free World, the first black president of the mightiest country in the world, sworn into office only a few months earlier. He was probably the most popular person in the world. His words mattered. It was also his first visit as President to an African country. The whole world paid attention to Obama's visit to Ghana, and his speech at the Ghanaian Parliament was dubbed 'Obama's historic message to Africa'. His words on that occasion mattered very much.

I experienced Obama's endorsement of the libellous reporter as an assault in much the same way as I experienced the media attacks. It was another blow. Obama may not have known of the libel and slander. He likely had not even heard of Anas prior to his arrival in Ghana. I am told he mispronounced Anas' full name. Still, those words of endorsement came out of Obama's own mouth. Besides, the American ambassador knew that I had the reporter and his editor-in-chief and co-conspirator in court for defamation.

There was private outrage of sorts in Ghana and elsewhere about Obama's curious endorsement of a reporter whose tactics are questionable at best and who was a defendant in a pending defamation suit. My favourite was the reaction of an administrative staff member at our offices in Accra: 'I thought there was an injunction against Anas and Kweku Baako for their actions against you; is Obama not in contempt of court?'

A high-level representative of a human rights body was also present at the function where Obama spoke. 'We did not like that at all,' she told me, referring to Obama's endorsement of Anas.

'There are renowned journalists in Ghana that Obama could have endorsed, not Anas,' said an acquaintance.

'They are trying to rehabilitate him,' said a London-based African journalist who had been taken aback by Obama's endorsement. They were trying to rehabilitate Anas because he had brought himself into disrepute by writing and speaking untruthfully about me. If Anas were not rehabilitated, he would be out of business because no one would believe his stories.

'Does Anas work for the Americans?' asked an acquaintance, who had been alarmed by Obama's praise of Anas. I do not know the answer to that, but one has to wonder what the American interest was in what at first glance seemed to be a local matter. According to the BBC and other credible sources, former Liberian president and convicted war criminal Charles Taylor worked for US intelligence in Liberia. Similarly, Human Rights Watch has revealed that convicted mass killer and torturer Hissène Habré, responsible for the murder of more than forty thousand people, was brought into power by the governments of France and the US under President Ronald Regan. The US provided him with training, arms and financing, and continued to support Habré's government 'even as it committed widespread and systematic human rights violations'. In doing so, the US enabled one of Africa's most violent dictators. So why not a serial libeller, a slanderer and a fabricator of lies? Significantly, the US was one of the strongest supporters of bringing both Taylor and Habré to justice eventually.

In a TED Talk, renowned author Chimamanda Adichie cautioned against the dangers of telling a single story. Single stories can be misleading. Therefore, I would like to heed her warning. America can of course be credited for having done great things. America liberated Europe from Nazi Germany. America's election to its presidency of a Kenyan American who answers to a Kenyan name is another example of America's greatness.

Mum's cousin, Professor Richard Turkson, an esteemed member of the ruling NDC party, had been at the function where Obama spoke. He too had been surprised by Obama's remarkable endorsement.

'What was he trying to do, encourage the Ghanaian youth to become vigilantes? Ignore it,' he said. He was encouraging me to rise above Obama's remarks. I certainly hope the Ghanaian youth will not be impressed by Anas' diabolical tactics and the dubious endorsement. Our country will not be helped by vigilantism. It will not bring progress.

Professor Turkson had been helpful years earlier during another NDC administration when African Perspectives convened a pan-African conference in Accra on 'Litigating Economic and Social Rights in Africa'. We'd written to the Attorney-General with a request for him to officiate at the meeting but got no response. One of our board members at the time said he had gone to school with the Attorney-General and so went to his office on a number of occasions in an attempt to speak with him; however, he got no audience. We decided to proceed without the Attorney-General.

However, some two weeks before the conference, Dad called to tell me that the Attorney-General had in fact agreed to open our conference.

'How did you arrange this, Dad? You don't know anyone in the government,' I said.

'Your mother's cousin is a respected member of the NDC party, and so we reached out to him,' Dad said. Professor Turkson had in turn reached out to the Minister for Local Government, who in turn contacted the Attorney-General to ask him to kindly officiate at our conference. He even accompanied the Attorney-General to the opening of our event. Dad always seemed to know what to do in difficult situations. I have often wondered if I would have been so disparaged in the media had Dad been alive. We were all so vulnerable after Dad passed.

Professor Turkson got to know of the libel much later because he had been out of the country. Besides, we had not even thought about involving him. He would later tell me and Mum how much he wished we'd involved him earlier when the threats began. The truth is that we did not expect things to get to that point.

He made some enquiries and was informed that Kweku Baako, regarded as a formidable media man and sympathiser of the erstwhile NPP government, had orchestrated the libel. He learned that Kweku Baako and Barbara Bonsu were old friends. Anas worked for Kweku Baako and so he put Anas up to writing the story. 'Those people went too far,' Uncle Richard said, baffled.

Another clansman also made some enquiries and was told by his contact in the NDC government that African Perspectives had been sued by the German Development Agency. Seriously, was that a reason to be attacked and lied about in the mass media? As already explained, GTZ in fact did an Amy Cooper job on African Perspectives. They did me and the organisation wrong. I hoped GTZ had not used its development aid power in Ghana to add another layer of politicisation to the dispute. The NDC representative also told the clansman that I was involved in another lawsuit. He was referring to the dispute with Paolo, the developer of the gated community's company. As if I was the only one suing them! There were so many lawsuits against Paolo and his company. Besides, it was not like I had taken the law into my own hands by hiring a mercenary. I believe in the rule of law even in a country where politics prevail over justice. When we lived in Ghana, we personally felt we needed to retain a lawyer to deal with the inevitable bullying and lawlessness that we were constantly confronted with. I don't even believe in being litigious. I know from my work as a human rights lawyer that litigation should be the last option for settling most disputes. Yet I was compelled to take the media men to court, just like I'd sued Paolo. Both the media men and Paolo were clearly influential in the NDC circles. It appears that Paolo and the media men were not pleased with my suits against them, but I had no other choice.

The plot the perpetrators used was probably more sinister than Kweku Baako simply helping his old friend Barbara Bonsu. Professor Turkson was probably unaware that Kweku Baako's old friend, known only as the owner of the Joint's Media Mafia, was also General Bonsu's wife. General Bonsu was working as special adviser to the newly elected President of Ghana, John Evans Atta Mills. General Bonsu had the state apparatus at his disposal, as is the case when people work in the seat of power in our still-developing democracy.

I have pondered if Kweku Baako, a renowned critic of the NDC's founder, Jerry Rawlings, was used as an intelligence scheme to divert suspicion and responsibility for the media assaults from the ruling government. Kweku Baako turned out not to be a critic of Mills' NDC government though.

My lawyer Godwin had initially approached a schoolmate of his who was working in the office of the newly appointed Attorney-General about the media assaults. The response of the Attorney-General's associate was revealing, almost rehearsed. He said that because Baako and his newspaper were known to be sympathetic to the NPP government, if the Attorney-General's Office took them on, it would look as if they were deliberately going against the opposition party. I got the impression that the associate was just repeating what he'd heard or had been told. Surely it wasn't up to him to decide whether to take on the media men or not. It was probably not up to the Attorney-General either. In our part of the world, such a decision – to prosecute or not to prosecute – is made at the highest level. However, the ailing President was deemed not to be in control of his government: those closest to him were.

In any case, the line of reasoning that the Attorney-General's Office could not get involved because Baako and his newspaper supported the opposition party does not persuade. The issue is not whether a suspect belongs to the opposition or ruling party. Rather, the issue is whether an offence has been committed, irrespective of political fraternity. Surely collaborators of the erstwhile NPP government would be held responsible for their offences, unless they were being used as frontline perpetrators to shield the masterminds in return for political favours.

Even after we had fled Ghana, the new Attorney-General, Betty Mould-Idrissu, still refused to intervene. She suggested that because Alhaji Mumuni, the new Foreign Minister, had implicated himself in the matter, her office could not get involved. In other words, they would not go against one of their own.

It is interesting that I was libelled and slandered under the regime of President Atta Mills, who was from the Ekumfi State, where my mother was the Paramount Queen Mother at the time. President Mills knew Mum, but only formally. He would walk over to greet her at Ekumfi and other functions. At one such function, shortly after we retreated to the Netherlands, Mum told him she'd like to meet with him to discuss a matter. Mum said he'd looked rather surprised, and said, 'Of course, Queen.' However, her attempts to meet with the President did not materialise. Mum later learned that there were people at the Presidency who knew that my mother was the Paramount Queen Mother of Ekumfi and made it their business to block any possible appointment with the President. There was also talk that we were among the Ekumfi people who were sympathetic to the rival NPP party.

Professor Turkson approached both the Foreign Minister and the Attorney-General about African Perspectives' headquarters agreement. They had both been surprised, because the perpetrators had branded me a staunch supporter of the NPP. I don't think NPP officials considered me as one of their own and I wasn't partisan in my work – which is how I got to know some of the politicians, through my work.

Through Professor Turkson's efforts and those of Edwin, a board member of African Perspectives, a meeting was held to discuss the headquarters agreement. Edwin and Anna Bossman met with the Foreign Minister. They reported that the meeting went well, and that the Foreign Minister was open to reinstating our headquarters agreement with some fine-tuning. The brothel story was not mentioned at the meeting. Macarious, the civil servant who had colluded with the perpetrators in spreading falsehoods that our headquarters agreement was fraudulently procured, was assigned as our organisation's contact for concluding the renewed agreement. By then Professor Turkson had been appointed ambassador to Canada and had begun his tour of duty there. Macarious failed to cooperate, and we did not try to bribe him because that's not what we do. Indeed, I have observed that mid-level civil servants in Ghana can in practice overrule even the decision of a president.

Sometime after we'd moved back to the Netherlands, Panyin and Kaakra became friendly with a girl in their new school. Fleur and her family had relocated to the Netherlands from South Africa. Her father's job with a multinational company had taken them to different countries. When Fleur learned of Panyin and Kaakra's Ghanaian origins, she told them she had lived in Accra and had attended the Roosevelt School. The girls were excited to learn that they had attended the same school during the same period. When Panyin and Kaakra visited Fleur, she showed them a yearbook from Roosevelt, which had their pictures in it. The girls brought the yearbook home to show us and asked why we did not have a copy. They were much younger and equally cute then. I had to tell them that we had left the yearbooks behind in Ghana.

Klaas-Jan and I were friendly with Fleur's parents. During a visit to their home, the subject of Obama's trip to Ghana came up. They had been living in Ghana during Obama's visit. Fleur's mother told me that Fleur had received an academic recognition from the school autographed by Obama himself. Did Obama have direct contact with Roosevelt officials during his visit? When George W. Bush had visited Ghana some seventeen months earlier, he had not gone to Roosevelt. He visited the Ghana International School, which uses the British curriculum. So perhaps this time around, it made sense for the American president to visit Roosevelt.

'Why did we leave Ghana again?' Kaakra asked. This was not the first time she'd asked, but perhaps she was asking again because the explanation I gave didn't make much sense to her. When she had asked a couple of years earlier, I told her it was because someone with government support had told horrible lies about me in the media.

'Did he write about me and Panyin too?' she had asked anxiously.

'No, of course not,' I'd replied.

'Thank goodness,' she had said with a sigh.

This time, when Kaakra asked why we'd left Ghana, it was Panyin who answered. 'It is because she was libelled.'

'What does libel mean?' Kaakra asked, as if she had not heard that word used in our house a thousand times.

'It is when someone tries to destroy your career,' Panyin said.

Panyin and Kaakra's new school in the Netherlands held a ceremony when the pupils completed primary school, complete with graduation robes. It was a colourful event showcasing the multicultural character of the school, which hosts students from more than one hundred different nationalities, with flags of the various countries on display. I was surprised to see the Ghanaian flag too.

'I didn't know there were Ghanaians in this school,' I said to Klaas-Jan.

'Panyin and Kaakra,' he said.

'Oh, so I'm responsible for the Ghanaian flag being here?'

The day she found out about the details of why we left Ghana, Panyin told me a story. It was about a conversation they'd had with some friends at their new school a couple of years after we moved back to the Netherlands. The topic of the conversation was, 'How did you find out you were moving to Holland?' The international school kids sometimes learned about their move to a new country rather suddenly, for example when a parent got a lucrative position in another country that required an immediate move. Panyin and Kaakra's story was rather unique. They told their friends they were watching a Disney film when we told them we had to leave.

'That sounds like a refugee story,' said one boy.

One of the girls in the group then told Panyin privately to ask her parents to tell her exactly what happened.

Our daughters learned the details of why we left Ghana when Panyin started reading the manuscript for this book. She came downstairs to the kitchen with the manuscript in hand, looking amused and amazed. 'Mummy, I didn't know you were accused of running a brothel.'

I told her that was why we'd left Ghana. I didn't feel safe. Besides, they would have been vulnerable in a school and country where their mother had been so horribly accused in the mass media. The front door opened and Kaakra came in. Panyin quickly went to tell her twin what she had just learned about my Amy Cooper moments.

8

MEDIA TYRANNY

INTERESTINGLY, CNN HAD SHORTLISTED ANAS for its 2009 African Journalist Awards. This was announced some months after we retreated to the Netherlands. Friends in Ghana told me that the Ghanaian evening news opened with an announcement of Anas' nomination.

That appeared to be another attempt to restore the image of the tabloid reporter I had in court for libel and slander. The unsubstantiated brothel allegations made by Anas, and my suit against him, had brought Anas' credibility into question. Therefore, the CNN nomination, like the Obama endorsement, perhaps sought to restore him to the reputation he enjoyed prior to my lawsuit. Notably, both CNN and Obama are American entities that may have been misused by people with access. What was the American interest, one may ask?

I also learned that Anas' nomination for a CNN award had been featured on the Ghana government's website with an accompanying story that Anas was tipped to win the award. What was the interest of the Ghana government? Would Anas' nomination have been featured on the government's website if he had been writing about the government too?

In an interview that seemed to have been procured from a former country correspondent for both the BBC and

Reuters, Kwaku Sakyi-Addo, shortly after I took Anas and Kweku Baako to court, the interviewer provided a platform for Anas to explain his working methods. He eulogised Anas at the beginning of the interview, praising and glorifying him. Anas' face was covered, allegedly for security reasons, because the stories he tells affect people's reputations. Yet he's the most profiled and fame-seeking undercover investigator there is. Quite a contradiction. It's not like people do not know what he looks like. His fellow journalists and the so-called Media Mafia at Barbara Bonsu's joint all know what he looks like. When I dragged him into court, the public did see him. Since then, Anas does not appear at official gatherings with his plain face – not even in courts. Shouldn't a judge be able to see who he claims to be in a closed-door session?

In any case, I didn't believe Anas had anything to fear in Ghana. He is known to be feared by the police. His modus operandi is based on blackmail, fabrications and entrapments by a private investigator, all of which would be treated as the violations they are in any civilised nation. He usually preys on those rendered defenceless because his activities are procured by the powers that be. However, in 2019, Anas' associate who had worked with him on some high-profile cases was shot dead by unidentified gunmen on motorbikes. There were suggestions that Anas feared for his life, and no one seemed to know where he was. This time, his media friends did not come to his rescue. They did not support him like they had done when I sued him.

In the 2009 interview with Kwaku Sakyi-Addo, Anas' awards were in the background of the shot. One of them was received in the presence of The Elders, among them former United Nations Secretary-General Kofi Annan. Those awards were being used as evidence that the brothel allegations he had made against me must be true. The brothel story was mentioned at the very end of the interview.

'What about the spa?' Sakyi-Addo asked, despite my application to the High Court for an injunction against Anas, Baako and their agents.

'I have evidence that will shock the nation,' Anas responded, despite my application for an injunction.

I believe any responsible and ethical journalist would have followed up with Anas to enquire about his evidence and why the evidence that would shock the nation was never produced.

Why had Sakyi-Addo not interviewed me about my work as a human rights lawyer like he had interviewed Anas as an investigative journalist? Why did he not ask me how I found myself in this controversy? That's what an independent journalist would have done. This journalist knew of me through African Perspectives and had attended at least one of our press conferences prior to a high-profile conference we held in Accra. What I have observed is that well-known journalists in Ghana tend to be more political than independent. There are barely a handful of seemingly independent journalists in this 'model African democracy'.

The media men also used their connections to put pressure on my lawyer. For example, after we filed the suit, and shortly after the High Court issued the injunction against the defendants, Godwin arrived at work one day and found an envelope on his desk. The letter in the envelope was entitled 'Ewurabena'. It was from a senior lawyer at the same law firm. Godwin's senior was a childhood friend of Kweku Baako, Anas' co-defendant and editor-in-chief. He told Godwin to drop the case or be sanctioned. He said both Baako and Anas were clients of their firm and therefore Godwin could not sue them. He would subsequently tell Godwin that his position would have been different if African Perspectives were to have given them cases. Godwin explained to me how their firm worked: each lawyer was self-employed and paid their part of the rent and other common costs. The lawyers brought in their own clients and exchanged ideas on legal issues but did not share profits. One of the lawyers had represented Anas briefly in a motor accident case some years back. The senior lawyer's demand that Godwin drop the case was rather hypocritical. I am told that he had himself sued a client of one of the firm's other lawyers. If he could sue a client of that firm, how could he then order Godwin not to sue Anas, who had only briefly been represented by one of the firm's lawyers? Godwin wrote a strongly worded response. He told his senior in no uncertain terms that he should have appreciated the harm done to me and African Perspectives. After the exchange with his senior, Godwin remained on the case, but the pressures did not stop.

When I first engaged Godwin, he disclosed to me that the defendants' lawyer – who was also Barbara Bonsu's lawyer – was married to his cousin. I believed that Godwin's family relationship with the defendants' lawyer would not pose a professional conflict because he did not seem to think much of him. However, one Saturday evening, Kweku Baako went round to his lawyer's house. The lawyer's wife called Godwin, her cousin. There's nothing wrong with calling a cousin on a Saturday evening, except that Godwin's cousin wanted him to speak to Baako, a co-defendant in the defamation suit. Baako was asking to speak with my lawyer. That evening Godwin resisted, but I could tell that the pressures were getting to him.

Godwin told me some of his friends, who were also friends of Anas, had stopped speaking to him because he was suing Anas. The media men also used Godwin's friends and colleagues to get to him. When African Perspectives' headquarters agreement was abruptly terminated without due process, the activist group Alliance for Accountable Governance (AFAG) staged a demonstration against the government and the Foreign Minister in particular. The spokesperson of the group was friendly with Godwin and told him Baako had approached him in reaction to their demonstration. Reportedly, Baako had invited him to his home and given him a screening of the pornographic video they had fabricated to claim that I was running a brothel. Yet Baako and his co-defendant Anas repeatedly failed to deposit the video in court when I sued. Showing the fabricated video to the spokesperson of AFAG was in clear violation of the order of injunction. This was not the defendants' only contemptible action. After I posted my letter to Obama on African Perspectives' website, asking him to retract his endorsement of Anas, the perpetrators, through their friends in the media, continued to assault and insult me in the mass media and online without consequence.

After showing the fabricated video to AFAG's spokesperson, Baako told him, 'If you really knew African Perspectives, you would not stand up for them.' What did their pornographic video have to do with the headquarters agreement between African Perspectives and the government of Ghana? Baako himself does not know African Perspectives, nor does he care to know about the niche we occupy in the world of human rights and international justice. He only wanted to disparage me further to cover up his offences. They had not expected me to call them to account when they told their manufactured story. They had expected me to go and smooth things out with them, and for the benefit of their friend, General Bonsu's wife. However, I had not responded in the way they had anticipated. I had not responded like a politician. I responded like the human rights advocate that I am and took them to court. I am told that a man who co-owned a newspaper that Baako previously worked for and knows Baako well made an interesting observation. He said Baako and Anas knew they would lose the case and so their strategy was to attack, assault, crash. He said he'd spoken to me, and heard the yearning for justice in my voice, and was confident that Baako and Anas would not succeed in their ploy. He was certain they would be exposed.

I have often wondered about Baako's brutality. Baako rose to national fame during the Rawlings era, when, in telling stories designed to oppose Rawlings' government, he was arrested and detained. According to him, he was incarcerated on three occasions. On one of those occasions, he was charged and convicted of criminal libel and served a prison sentence. He says he was tortured while in detention and has told some graphic stories about his experiences and those of his fellow inmates. I do not know if those allegations have been proven, but they were believed in the court of public opinion. If true, did those experiences dehumanise Baako? Is this the victim-turned-perpetrator syndrome? Former President Rawlings has denied those allegations made by Baako. Around mid-2020, Baako extended an olive branch to Jerry Rawlings, which the former President rejected, saying Baako had peddled falsehoods about him.

As for Anas, I do not know what his story is, but I was intrigued to learn that his father was a soldier. I can imagine that a controlled professional soldier could teach positive life lessons to his children. Lessons of strength, discipline and resilience. On the other hand, an undisciplined, unloving soldier father could do just the opposite to his children and by extension to society at large.

After viewing the pornographic video, the AFAG spokesperson went to Godwin and asked him to drop the case. He had fallen for their fabricated story. Godwin had already seen the video before filing the suit. He had been interviewed on national television together with Kweku Baako when I sued Anas and Baako. The interviewer said in her introduction, 'The executive director of African Perspectives, the lady at the centre of the Working Girl Wellness controversy, has called the bluff of ace investigative journalist Anas Aremeyaw Anas and taken him to court.' Godwin told the interviewer that the video was a fabrication. A respected media lawyer, Godwin told the interviewer that he normally defended the freedom of the press, but this time he was going against the media. A media person who knows Baako well and had watched the interview said he could tell Baako was nervous; he didn't have a defence. Rather, Baako responded that they would fight the case in the court of public opinion. That was meant as a threat for starting the case against them. But why would they not fight the case in the law courts with the 'evidence that would shock the nation'?

Klaas-Jan had taken Anas' pornographic video with him to a media house in the Netherlands for review. They dismissed it as a fabrication. Klaas-Jan told me how they had analysed the video, how you could clearly see that the video had been shot at different locations and copied and pasted into a single video. I wanted to view the video in this professional setting for myself, and so when I went to the Netherlands during the Easter break, I visited the media house. The man analysing the video in the screening room couldn't stop laughing. I might have laughed too if it was not so evil. If the people behind it all were not filled with hate.

'This is a very strange video,' the man in the screening room said over and over as he laughed.

I had watched the video in Accra when Godwin gave it to me, but the details were clearer in the screening room of the media house. In the video, a woman whose face was blurred, and alleged to be a therapist at Working Girl Wellness Centre, was massaging the penis of a man, the alleged diplomat, whose face was partly covered with a cloth over the eyes and around the back of his head. It might have appeared persuasive if the so-called diplomat had appeared foreign. Even though his eyes were covered you could see that he looked like a local: his forehead, his jaws, his chin. He also sounded like a local from his groans.

The Citi FM journalist who had called me about a month earlier, on the day the libellous article was published, had told me he'd asked Anas why the diplomat's eyes were covered. Anas responded that they did not want to expose him because he was a diplomat. But wasn't the whole exercise to expose diplomats caught in sex scandals? The journalist also told me that after Anas left their studio, he and his colleague looked at each other in disbelief, and then he said to his colleague, 'I think this time Anas made a mistake.' But how could he make an innocent mistake with a fabricated video he had produced himself? Anas and his co-perpetrators committed a premeditated and malicious offence.

Anas had claimed that the sex scene had been caught on tape by a hidden camera, but in fact the cameraman was in the room. You could see the camera moving, and then it would stop right where the sexual act was taking place, to get a good shot of it before filming from other angles. You could also see that the video had been shot in different locations. One location was dark, while the other was lighter, and one ceiling was higher than the other. Anas had claimed that he had investigated Working Girl Wellness Centre for five months. And what did he have to show for five months of his ace investigation? A fabricated video.

I asked the man in the screening room at the media house in the Netherlands if he'd be prepared to fly to Accra and explain the video in court. He said he would. I am quite sure there are capable technicians in Ghana who could explain the video, but they would be pressured by the media men and corrupt politicians. They would be bought. I was determined to have the video played in court, to expose its flaws. But the defendants did all they could to prevent the suit from moving forward.

Gender literary expert Dr Pinkie Mekgwe coined the term 'media rape' when she wrote about the way I had been repeatedly assaulted in the media. Her article entitled 'When the Media Becomes a Weapon of War Against Gender Progress' was published on the Genderlinks website. Shortly thereafter, it was splashed on the internet that Anas had been invited by the UN Commission on the Status of Women to participate in a panel discussion at the UN Headquarters in New York. So, the investigative reporter who had defamed me in a gendered manner – by playing on the name Working Girl and thereby claiming I was running a brothel – was now an expert on the rights of women. Who was promoting Anas, and what was their interest? It was another attempt to rehabilitate the libellous reporter.

Around that same time, Anas came out with a video showing Ghana's customs officials accepting bribes. This time eyebrows were raised, and some Ghanaian journalists questioned how Anas had managed to obtain unprecedented access to highly secured and sensitive places. The government later admitted that they had in fact given Anas access to secured places that were off-limits. Why, one may ask, was this the case? Can an investigative journalist sponsored by the government be deemed independent? Does Ghana not have the proper structures in place to catch corrupt officials? Shouldn't Ghana be building a strong security and police force instead of resorting to 'strong men' like Obama advised? How far would they go to try to rehabilitate the perpetrator? Did my case against Anas pose such a threat? Would it threaten his work for powerful forces if Anas were to be exposed for the mercenary that he is? I suppose among unruly people, anyone with an independent mind would pose a threat. My wise friend, hundred-plus-year-old Benjamin Ferencz, the last surviving prosecutor of the Nuremberg Trials, has observed that 'you cannot kill an ideology.' Yes, indeed. Nor can you kill the ideal of an independent mind.

9

A LETTER TO CNN

ABOUT A WEEK AFTER OBAMA'S SPEECH, ANAS left for the Indian Ocean city of Durban in South Africa to attend the CNN MultiChoice African Journalist Awards ceremony, armed with the backing of the most powerful man on earth. The award would be lucrative for Anas: a stint at the CNN headquarters, a cash payment, not to mention the recognition that would come with the award, which he would make much noise about and use as a cover for his dubious and false stories.

Anas had received some obscure awards in the past, but I didn't mind. That said, one such award that he supposedly received did cause me to raise my eyebrows. The award had been established by the then President of Burkina Faso, Blaise Compaoré, and Anas was the first recipient. It is notable that the first of this award would go to a national of an English-speaking country, when Burkina Faso is a French-speaking country. Compaoré is not known for his human rights record, so he can give Anas all the awards he wants. His name comes up from time to time in human rights and international criminal justice circles, where his alleged role in the Sierra Leonean conflict is often mentioned along with those of Muammar al-Qaddafi of Libya and Charles Taylor of Liberia. He was forced to flee his country in the 2014 Burkinabé uprising and has since been living in exile in Ivory

Coast. Speaking of fleeing, there are two types: fleeing from injustice, like I did, and fleeing from justice, like dictators, corrupt politicians and enemies of humankind do.

A principled and independent journalist would instead write about Compaoré's rights violations and decline the award. Of course, it may be that this award too was procured in an attempt to rehabilitate Anas, whose job and livelihood were dependent on people believing his stories. Pity that Obama and Compaoré now have something in common – they are both Anas endorsers. Obama must have been tricked. Curiously, that award has disappeared from the Ghanaian media websites that previously announced it. Could it be that after the 2014 Burkinabé uprising that forced Compaoré to flee his country, it was deemed politically incorrect for Anas to flaunt that award, and instead better for him to pretend to have never received such an award?

The only other time that Compaoré's name had come up so out of the blue was in connection with the gated community where we'd purchased a home. The daughter of the developer, who held an executive position at the company, had suggested that we meet her mother, who was an interior designer. This was earlier in our relationship before we sued them and before Paolo would tell our mutual friend Erica that her friendship with me posed a conflict of interest. Klaas-Jan and I had no plans to hire an interior decorator, but we decided to meet with her anyway. We were curious to see what an interior decorator's home looked like. We met with her at her home, outside the gate in the community. Her living room was ultra-minimalist, so bare and not our style. She told us she had returned from Burkina

Faso that morning. She had gone there to decorate the presidential palace. So, years later, after Anas defamed me and I learned that he had been given an award by the dictator of Burkina Faso not long after that, I remembered what Paolo's ex-wife told us when we visited her house some years back: that she had decorated Compaoré's palace. Did Paolo's family know Compaoré?

Still, Anas could be given obscure awards, but no, he could not, and should not, win the CNN MultiChoice African Journalist Award. It would be another violation, another injustice. I called CNN in subtle protest when I learned of Anas' nomination. I informed Caroline Creasy, the contact person for the award in 2009, that Anas had libelled and slandered me in the mass media. She suggested that I speak to their representative in Ghana, Edward Boateng. It turned out he was the initiator of the award. That was a surprise. I knew Edward Boateng; we lived in the same community. He was married to President Kufuor's niece and Kufuor had appointed him chair of the US-funded Millennium Development Authority (MIDA) in Ghana. I remember having been informed that the Roosevelt School principals, who worked at MIDA or had connections there, had asked Boateng, who had ties with the Ghana government, to assist with the school's resident and work permit issues for expatriate teachers. Boateng was not a Roosevelt parent though.

We had a more direct connection as homeowners in the community, exploring how best to solve our land title issues collectively. I advocated for a legal approach, while Boateng advocated for a media approach. Still, it didn't even occur to me that he was a media man. The last time I'd seen him was when I invited him to an informal reception at our home. I had asked him to help my younger brother Aboagye, who was visiting Ghana with his course mates from Harvard, to get an audience at the Presidency. The reception was an opportunity for them to meet Boateng. During the reception, Boateng mentioned to me that his brother had purchased a house in the gated community and had moved there. I guessed he'd solved his land title issues with Paolo.

Surely Boateng must have heard about the media accusations against me. If he was the CNN African Journalist Awards' representative in Ghana, then had he supported Anas' nomination? He must have. I would later learn that he had even commended Obama's endorsement of Anas. What was going on? Had he not heard that Anas had accused me in the media of running a brothel? Did he believe those wild accusations? Was it just a coincidence that he was chairing the US-funded MIDA and supporting Anas' nomination for a CNN African Journalist Award? Was it a coincidence that Paolo, the developer he had once wished to take on through the media, had now sold a house to Boateng's brother? Was it a coincidence that one of the MIDA officials was one of the Americans on the Roosevelt school board, and that the husband of Froukje, the former vice-chair of the school board, was also a senior official at MIDA? And what about Paolo the developer, who incidentally was a member of the Roosevelt community?

When Caroline Creasy suggested I approach the representative of the CNN MultiChoice African Journalist Awards in Accra, I informed her that I knew Edward

Boateng because we lived in the same community. I told her I would much rather submit a formal complaint to CNN, and that I'd been informed that Anas was feared by many in Ghana, including the police. I could almost feel her shudder at the other end of the phone, for why would the police be afraid of an investigative journalist? She asked me to send my complaint to her and assured me she'd forward it to a CNN vice-president. It was comforting to know from the name that the vice-president to whom my complaint would be sent was a woman.

My complaint to CNN against Anas Aremeyaw Anas was both in my personal capacity and as the executive director of African Perspectives. I informed CNN about my suit for defamation against Anas and Kweku Baako. I told them that I am a human rights lawyer with academic and practical legal experience in North America, Europe and Africa, and had various publications to my name, including four scholarly books.

I expressed concerns about Anas' CNN nomination, which he has exploited as part of his media campaign to disparage me. Even though he has no evidence to substantiate his allegations, Anas has sought to misuse the recognition he enjoys to mislead the public to believe that the stories he wrote about me were true. I questioned the criteria for giving awards to reporters, which appears to be whether they had told a 'good' story, and not whether the story was true, the evidence real, and the minimum standards for reporting met. I intimated that those omissions were worrisome in the context of Africa, where compliance with basic standards is *not* the order of the day.

I informed CNN about two other dubious stories I learned Anas has told involving a biscuit factory and a plastic company, and my belief that Anas is an ingenious mercenary, a hatchet man, whose services are procured to disparage, if not destroy, the opponents of those who hire and pay him. I highlighted the flaws in Anas' article against me. For example, it discusses in general terms issues concerning sex tourism and pornography in Ghana and includes pictures of naked women taken from certain websites. His so-called evidence to substantiate his claim that I was running a brothel is one video tape, where a woman, supposedly an employee of the spa whose face cannot be seen, is massaging the penis of a so-called diplomat whose face is covered. I notified CNN about Anas' claim that they had 'evidence that would shock the nation' and yet repeatedly failed to tender their evidence in court.

I told them about the multiplier effect of the libel and its reach worldwide because Anas and Baako's fabricated story and video were posted on the internet, and that this was especially damaging to me because of my international profile. I informed CNN that Anas' article against me had clearly targeted African Perspectives' headquarters agreement, which was withdrawn by the government.

I told CNN about the role of Barbara Bonsu, her relationship with the defendants, as well as her government and military connections. I let CNN know about the defendants' lawlessness, including continuing to write and speak untruthfully about me, using their fabricated video as a lobbying tool against me, Working Girl Wellness Centre and African Perspectives. I apprised them of Anas and his co-perpetrators' persistent efforts to mislead the public, in spite of my pending application for an injunction, in flagrant violation of the rules of court. These included the interview with Kwaku Sakyi-Addo, and a subsequent article Anas and Baako published claiming that Working Girl had been closed down, when they knew it had not, but had instead been illegally seized by Barbara Bonsu and her co-conspirators as part of Anas and Baako's scheme. Anas wanted to mislead the public to believe that Working Girl had been closed down by the authorities as a result of his article, thereby suggesting that his false and fabricated story was substantiated.

I informed CNN about the fact that front-page articles, even from the smaller tabloids, are repeated every evening in *News Brief*, the highlights of the day's news in Ghana. Consequently, as a result of Anas' second publication claiming the spa had closed down, the country was misled into believing that that was indeed the case. I also informed them that Anas and Baako were putting pressure on my lawyer to drop the defamation action I brought against them and had lobbied his colleagues and friends, and that Anas had personally approached my lawyer in an attempt to coerce and intimidate me into not pursuing justice. Anas had told my lawyer that if he, Anas, were to win an award, presumably in reference to the CNN nomination, my application for an injunction would prevent him from discussing me. I also told CNN about Anas and Baako's misuse of legal processes to stop the case from moving forward.

Last but not least, I let CNN know about the consequences of Anas' actions on my family, in particular our seven-year-old daughters. As a result of Anas' false story, my husband and I had to withdraw our children from the international school they had attended for two years and where they had made many friends. I had been elected to the school board and chaired the policy and regulations committee that amended the constitution. Because of my involvement in the governance of the school, and perhaps coupled with the fact that I was the only Ghanaian on the board, my name was a recognisable one at the school. It was therefore not surprising that Anas' article about me was a subject of discussion within the school. It was discussed not only by staff and parents but also among the students. My husband and I were especially concerned that discussions of the false allegations about their mother running a brothel would make our daughters vulnerable. As we could not protect them from the scandal, we felt we had no choice than to uproot them and move back to the Netherlands, at least temporarily, with the result that their education was disrupted before they could start their new school.

In conclusion, I told CNN that Anas' publication of the 20th of March 2009 had one purpose only: to disparage and cause harm to me.

After I e-mailed the letter, I followed up with Caroline Creasy. She cautioned me that she could not promise anything, which made me wonder whether the decision had already been taken to give Anas the award. However, I was persistent. I followed up again and again, wanting to know if my complaint was being considered. Caroline Creasy assured me she had sent the letter to the vice-president. Not too long after that, I received an e-mail from the chair of the panel responsible for the awards, a man with a Nigerian- or

Cameroonian-sounding last name. He said they had received my complaint. However, Anas' nomination was for a different story. Besides, since the story Anas told about me was in court, it would be *sub judice* for them to go into it. In other words, because the matter was under judicial consideration, they were prohibited from appraising it, or at the very least it would be inappropriate for them to do so. This is a rule Obama did not obey when he endorsed the defendant in his speech before the Ghanaian Parliament.

As luck would have it, the chair's message came around the same time as the High Court granted my request for an injunction. I wrote back to the chair of the panel and thanked him for his attention. I informed him about the court order enjoining Anas and his co-perpetrator and their agents from writing and speaking about me. I also informed him that while I could appreciate that they could not go into a matter before the courts, I was concerned that Anas would use an award from a reputable media house like CNN as evidence that his fabricated stories were true. In other words, a CNN award, regardless of which story the award was based on, would give him credibility for every story he told, including the fabricated stories. The gist of my message was that CNN could not and should not be an enabler. The chair of the panel wrote back immediately, thanking me for my response, and wishing me well.

'He will not get the award,' Klaas-Jan said.

My husband tuned in to watch the CNN awards ceremony on television. I could not bring myself to watch it.

'Don't worry, he will not win,' he reiterated.

He had also been confident that Anas and Baako would end up in jail when their fabricated brothel story broke. Rather, they became heroes because they had government support. This sorry state of affairs reminds me of an observation made by a family friend from the Netherlands, Mr Knobel, who had lived in Ghana for many years with his family. He was referring to a failed coup attempt during the Rawlings era. 'When they succeed in staging a rebellion, they become heroes, but when they fail, they are traitors,' he had said.

Klaas-Jan watched the CNN awards ceremony only up until a certain point. He came upstairs to tell me what he had heard at the beginning of the programme. Edward Boateng, the CNN Africa representative, had addressed the audience and said he was glad his countryman, Anas, had made it to the finals. Klaas-Jan interpreted this to mean that Anas would not win the award. Still, I was nervous. Klaas-Jan, who'd gone back downstairs, came back up after some time to tell me that Anas had in fact not won. It was such a relief.

'Let him continue with his tricks. Let him continue to chase awards and seek dubious endorsements. In the process he'll expose himself,' my reflective husband said.

I called my Mum to give her the news that Anas had not won the CNN award and she could not have been more relieved. Imagine if he had. He and his editor-in-chief and co-conspirator Kweku Baako, and all those he worked for, would have made sure it was world news.

A dear friend had a good reminder for me: 'Ewurabena, be content with the victories,' she said. Those victories she was referring to included the Accra High Court's injunction, which the perpetrators failed to obey, and of course the anticipated CNN award that Anas did not win.

I have wondered what CNN officials who knew about my complaint against Anas thought about Obama's endorsement of Anas just before the upcoming CNN awards ceremony. Dr Pinkie Mekgwe, the gender literary expert who wrote 'When the Media Becomes a Weapon of War against Gender Progress', told me a colleague had asked her who the journalist that Obama had endorsed in his 'message to Africa' was. She quickly sent her colleague my statement on the defamation, which was similar to but not exactly my complaint to CNN. About a year after the awards ceremony, African Perspectives and a Kenyan justice group organised a workshop in Nairobi. One of the participants pointed a Kenyan man out to me. He was the winner of the 2009 CNN African Journalist Award, the one Anas had expected to win. I just smiled, thinking to myself, 'There is a God'.

I decided to call my lawyer to tell him Anas had not got the CNN award. Godwin had been under so much pressure to drop the case that he was showing signs of caving in. He had been keen to represent me when I was libelled because he felt strongly that an injustice had been done to me, and I had engaged him because he had expertise in media cases. I liked the fact that he was young, barely thirty, too young to have become part of a corrupt system. He was a fine lawyer and an activist. However, he might not have appreciated the political realities of practising law in Ghana's seemingly developing democracy. Neither did I.

After I shared the news that Anas had not won the award, Godwin said in a low tone: 'Guess who called me this morning?'

'Who?' I asked.

'Anas,' he said. 'He was lamenting that my client had cost him the CNN award, which everyone said he'd win. He said you wrote to CNN to complain about him.'

I, of course, had informed Godwin of my complaint to CNN objecting to Anas' nomination.

'He has a lawyer, so he should have his lawyer call you instead of speaking with you directly,' I said.

'But I told you, we were in the same hall at university,' he replied.

In his sorrow, Anas told Godwin that he had interviewed me before publishing his scandalous article. He told Godwin he recorded the interview. Why was he only bringing that up now? Why had he not made that submission before the law courts? I wish he'd broadcast his so-called interview, but he wouldn't because it would implicate him. This so-called interview was the phone call we had about a month prior to the first wave of media attacks. I'd asked him what his interest was in the dispute between the spa and Barbara Bonsu. Was he trying to impress Barbara Bonsu in return for free food and drinks at her joint? He flipped, threatened me, and hung up the phone. Whoever heard of an interviewer fleeing during an interview?

Anas also complained to Godwin about my writing to Obama and then said: 'Why don't you ask your client to go to the National Media Commission? They'll ask me to retract and then I'll retract.'

This is how Godwin told me he'd responded to Anas' phone call: 'An injustice has been done to my client. I am her lawyer in Ghana only, and so I do not know what other actions she will take elsewhere. The best thing you can do is to make an unqualified retraction.'

That unqualified retraction has not been made, nor have Anas and Kweku Baako been called to account. I suspect the pressures on Godwin to drop the case increased after Anas lost the CNN award and following my letter to Obama.

Godwin eventually withdrew from the case because I refused to go to Ghana to testify on my own behalf, preferring to do so through a power of attorney. Klaas-Jan was opposed to me going to Ghana – at least not until the suit had come to its logical conclusion and the perpetrators been found liable, or until I had told my story, which I had started to write, whichever came first.

'Those perpetrators did not achieve what they set out to do; if you go, they'll plant drugs in your luggage,' he said.

John, the lawyer who represented Working Girl in its contempt of court application against Barbara Bonsu, had been successful in securing a conviction. However, his petition for a custodial sentence had been denied. Barbara Bonsu committed an offence against the administration of justice but was not punished for it. Nevertheless, the conviction alone was significant, and many had been surprised that we had got one at all, particularly when her husband, the General, was in government.

John told me that during the contempt proceedings he sensed from the judge's demeanour that he would be inclined not to convict the General's wife for contempt. 'I will not allow it,' he said. 'The judge is my junior at the bar. I will ensure that he adheres to the law.'

But after the contempt proceedings, he called me and announced with great satisfaction: 'Barbara Bonsu has been convicted for contempt of court. Ewurabena, you continue with your human rights work, and let Barbara Bonsu continue to sell her fried rice and chicken,' he added.

Having seized Working Girl and its premises while an Accra High Court was seized of the matter, Barbara Bonsu was ordered to return the premises and given a warning. Bonsu's lawyer was so relieved that his client was not given the custodial sentence John had asked for that, I am told, he blessed the judge: 'Live long my Lord, live long.'

Seba was ecstatic. Calm and prayerful by nature, she had anticipated victory and went to court that morning dressed in the victory colours of red and white. She led a team of people to the premises to receive the spa's contents from Bonsu. Some of the items were damaged and one of the Working Girl signboards was either not returned or could not be found. Seba had her helpers remount the remaining signboard above the entrance. The text was quite original, inspired by a basic human rights principle and my love of spa treatments. The sign read: 'We Offer You The Last Freedom: The Right To Escape Into Tranquillity'.

Seba wanted everyone to know that the stories told about the spa were false. She couldn't wait to call her clients, perhaps even purchase airtime on the radio to announce that Working Girl was open for treatments. I of course was glad that we had been vindicated. However, not many people knew about the court's decision. It was hardly publicised. It was not announced in the tabloids that had published the brothel story. It was certainly not announced by Kwaku Sakyi-Addo, the former local BBC and Reuters correspondent who had interviewed Anas shortly after I took him and Baako to court, praising and glorifying him. I suspect that Anas, Baako and their agents and allies did their best to prevent the court decision from being reported on and broadcast.

To get the word out about the decision in our favour, my friend, the African journalist based in London, issued a press release, which Seba circulated to media houses in Ghana and I among my networks. John told me he got a call from a journalist enquiring about the court decision, which he confirmed, adding that he was the lawyer who prosecuted the contempt of court charge against Barbara Bonsu. I also sent the press release about the court decision in our favour to the US ambassador, Donald Teitelbaum. Not too long after that, I received an invitation from the US Embassy to attend an event they were hosting. I wrote to the ambassador to inform him that I had left Ghana because of the media attacks. I also told him that even if I were in Ghana, I would not have accepted the invitation.

I had a decision to make: to continue or not to continue with Working Girl? If we reopened, people would get to know Anas and Baako's story for what it was: a terrible lie and propaganda. It would serve them right. Besides, Seba was ready to take over. A cousin in Accra encouraged me to reopen. 'Don't give in to their bullying,' she said. As for Mum, I think she was conflicted, mainly because Seba, her favourite great-niece, wanted it so badly. My younger brother, on the other hand, advised me against it: 'Sister Ewurabena, do not reopen it. It's simply not worth it.' He was right. Klaas-Jan had some chilling words that ended my contemplation: 'What if you get a call from Ghana one day that Seba's body has been found at Working Girl?' Klaas-Jan truly believed we were dealing at that level.

So in the end, I decided not to reopen Working Girl and Seba did not get her spa. But she did go back to school to earn a bachelor's degree in hospitality and tourism. She also met a fine man and is now married with three lovely children of her own.

John took over the libel case after Godwin withdrew. John had earlier told me about Anas' dubious stories, having represented another one of Anas' victims in a previous case. John had been determined to pursue my case, but it became clear that the media men had put pressure on him too. He once told me that after a court hearing during which he mentioned the Roosevelt School, Kweku Baako approached him to ask if he could send one of his reporters to interview him to learn more about the issues with Roosevelt. Having information against Roosevelt would be very lucrative for Baako and Anas. The defendants did all they could to prevent my suit from moving forward. In fact, earlier in the legal proceedings the defendants had been fined for their abuse of court processes. Then, somehow the scheduled hearings for the libel case kept getting postponed. Later, when I was finally able to reach John, he told me the case had been struck out of court due to it having been unduly prolonged.

The media tyrants had got their way. A Ghanaian friend would later tell me: 'Ewurabena, have you ever heard of a case in Ghana reaching its logical conclusion?'

And let's not forget that this was a highly politicised case, with Barack Obama even making an appearance.

10

THE FAT SURGEON

MY WEIGHT GOT OUT OF CONTROL AFTER THE media assaults. Sometimes acquaintances I had not seen for some time would literally not recognise me. This was the case when I attended the first Review Conference of the International Criminal Court in Kampala. I was sitting around a table in one of the large tents in the gardens of the venue at the conference. The government of Uganda offered lunch to some four thousand six hundred conference delegates, including representatives of states, inter-governmental and non-governmental organisations. Betty, a woman I knew from the human rights and international justice landscape, was sitting across the table chatting with some of the delegates. I hadn't seen her for some years, and as she was busy chatting with others, I didn't think I should interrupt. She saw me when I walked into the tent and joined the group around the large table but had said nothing. I figured we would have time to catch up at some point during the Review Conference.

She looked in my direction again. 'Ewurabena!' She had not recognised me earlier.

We had one-on-one time several months later in her native Kenya, when we hung out at the Westgate Shopping Mall in Nairobi, after African Perspectives' ICC complementarity workshop. She told me that when she saw me in Kampala, she was sure something had happened to me, or that perhaps I had given birth again, to another set of twins.

I had tried various diets. Sometimes I'd lose weight only to gain more weight. I needed help and help was on the way. I felt exhilarated when Klaas-Jan drove me to a small town in Belgium for an appointment with a surgeon. We'd never been to this part of Belgium. It looked more like Germany. That is what I loved about living in the quaint city of Maastricht, a city connecting three countries at the southern tip of the Netherlands. In just a matter of minutes you were in another culture. Even the restaurants – Thai, Chinese, Indian – were somewhat different. I asked Klaas-Jan if he was hungry.

'I am starving, I didn't eat breakfast,' he said.

My appointment was at eleven AM. I figured we should be done around noon. 'Why don't we have lunch in this town? Chinese?' I asked.

'Sure. You know I love Chinese,' he said.

I decided I was going to order a glass of white wine with my meal.

I couldn't wait for our meeting, and to meet this person who was about to change my life. I couldn't believe that in just one more week… Well, perhaps in two weeks, because I'd need a bit of time to recover. I was told the procedure was fairly simple though. You'd go into the hospital in the morning and leave in the evening. It was incredible. I'd be able to shop in all my favourite shops and wear my favourite clothes again. I'd visit a few shops in Belgium too. Maybe I'd go to Antwerp with Edith and some of the girls in The

Hague. I couldn't remember the last time I really enjoyed shopping for clothes. I'd go for casual, chic everyday suits. Mostly pant suits, and a few short skirts. I'd also sign up for another set of endermologie treatments to keep my skin firm and retaining its natural glow. I'd continue to do my oxygen facials every other week. What more could a girl ask for? I'd have it all.

'Should I tell Esi?' I asked Klaas-Jan.

'Why not?' he said.

Esi was my diet partner. She had moved from Accra to Geneva after her husband was posted there. We encouraged each other via telephone and Skype conversations. We'd both blown our diets again. Esi and I became friends in Ghana. Our daughters went to the Roosevelt School, and her husband Kojo and I are probably related: Mum's uncle was also Kojo's uncle, but we have not quite figured out the family connection. Mum was going to find out.

I thought about Rima, a legal adviser at one of the tribunals in The Hague. She lived in Mönchengladbach and commuted to work from Germany to the Netherlands, staying overnight, one to two nights a week. She was past thirty-five and was trying to conceive. She needed to lose some weight. She'd already lost fifteen kilos though. Rima is a beautiful person, kind-hearted, with a beautiful face. I decided to share this bit of magic with her – a quick and easy way out of our being trapped in our bodies.

We had a number of questions for the surgeon, who I was referred to by a general practitioner. I felt so blessed that this meeting was arranged only the day before, when others had to wait two months to see a surgeon with such expertise.

I was scheduled to see the surgeon outside his normal visiting hours. The surgery itself would occur six days later. I couldn't wait.

There was a health risk, and at the time I understood that the costs of the treatment would be covered by my health insurance, which is why I had to have the initial meeting with the surgeon to take pictures of the relevant body parts for prior authorisation by the insurance company. I remember thinking to myself, 'Thank God this is not America.' I wondered if Obamacare would cover such a procedure.

When we moved to Ghana some six years earlier, I was a perfect sixty-four kilos, not bad for my medium frame and height of one hundred and sixty-seven centimetres. By the time we left Ghana I was eighty-three kilos. My GP told me to lose weight. 'You have to live long,' he said. But instead, I gained even more. I had not gone back to my GP because I was embarrassed. I checked my blood pressure regularly though, and it was fine.

An acquaintance told me about liposuction. I went on the internet to read about it. It's a procedure where fat is sucked out of the problem areas, in my case my tummy and my arms. I called my GP in Belgium and asked if it was dangerous.

'Could I die from it?' I enquired.

'It is a fairly simple procedure,' he said. 'It will be good for you, but afterwards you must eat healthily and exercise regularly. Let's talk about it.'

I figured it was more dangerous to carry all that excess weight on my belly than to get liposuction. Klaas-Jan agreed. Besides, we trust the doctors in Belgium.

We arrived at the surgeon's practice. It looked like he lived there too, upstairs. A lady welcomed us. She was the surgeon's wife and secretary. This was quite common. She used to work in a neighbouring city until she met the doctor and they married, so we learned within minutes. I noticed her perfectly flat tummy. I saw her slight back rolls as she turned towards her desk. Her breasts were full and round. She looked very well maintained. When she left the waiting room and Klaas-Jan and I were alone, I asked him, 'Do you think she's had liposuction? Her tummy is flat, and didn't she say she had a two-and-a-half-year-old?'

Klaas-Jan had not noticed her flat tummy. He had not noticed her full, round breasts either. I believed him. He would have told me if he had noticed. I would love to have a tummy like that. I used to, back in the day.

The surgeon invited us to his office. He was not exactly thin. I noticed his big belly, which was almost as high as his chest. His body language was not friendly. There was a radio in his office with loud music on. He spoke very loudly, which was necessary because of the loud music.

'How much do you weigh?' he asked. I told him. He wrote it down.

'How old are you?' I told him. He wrote it down too.

'You need to lose thirty kilos and you cannot do it with liposuction. You'd die if that much fat was sucked out of your body unless you did a series of surgeries, which I do not recommend. To minimise the risk, we do not take out more than five litres of fat per surgery. And by the way,' he said, 'at your weight, it would be too risky to put you to sleep.'

He said he'd have to use local anaesthesia. He also explained that he does not take away weight, rather he shapes the body. He told me categorically that if I wanted to lose weight, I had two options. I could go on a diet with a lot of psychological support to understand the real reasons behind my weight gain. I knew what the real issues were. It was the stress of media violence. Alternatively, he said, I could get gastric bypass surgery, for which he could recommend a fine surgeon. He recommended the latter because he didn't believe I could lose weight without surgical assistance. He also said the surgery, which would be a big one, would not take away the weight either. It would only tighten my stomach so that I could not eat too much. I guess that is what you do to people with no self-control.

I'd heard rumours about an acquaintance who had had a gastric bypass and then gained all the weight back. I also believed I should be able to enjoy healthy meals without artificial restrictions on the quantity. I lost fifteen kilos all on my own after I had Panyin and Kaakra, just by reading a book and not just applying its principles, but also having a certain thought process about food. I actually quite enjoyed my meals then. I even lost five kilos during a three-week vacation in Italy without feeling deprived. I had recommended the book to others just as it had been recommended to me, and they'd seen immediate results too. Why couldn't I apply the same principles and logic of the book this time?

'If you do not get this surgery you are bound to die prematurely,' he said. 'And if those breasts are yours, I'd recommend a breast reduction.'

'Don't go there,' I thought to myself. 'If they are not mine, whose breasts are they? His wife may have had a boob job, but mine are real.'

'Could you turn down the radio? It is difficult to hear,' I said to him.

He turned down the radio and continued: 'You will develop back pain with those breasts. You will require a knee and hip replacement in due course at this weight. At this rate, your mobility will be affected, and you will end up in a wheelchair. I recommend gastric bypass surgery.'

He took a scrap of paper and wrote down the name of a specialist and handed it to Klaas-Jan. We looked at each other in disbelief. Was this man crazy?

'Think about it for two weeks,' the doctor said as we got up to leave.

On our way to the car, we did not talk about the lunch we were planning to have at a Chinese restaurant. We got in the car and drove straight home.

'I didn't know Belgians could be so blunt. He sounds like a doctor from Amsterdam,' Klaas-Jan said.

'It sounds like I am in trouble if I do not do something about my weight,' I replied.

'Let's forget about his attitude and think about his advice. He probably chose this method to get the message across, to shock you into action,' Klaas-Jan said.

'I am shocked all right, but there will be no gastric bypass surgery for me. Didn't he say that they could not put me under general anaesthesia at this weight anyway? Who ever heard of getting gastric surgery under local anaesthesia?' I replied.

When we arrived home, I walked in the freezing cold to a health shop not too far away. I bought vegetable juices and walnuts for the umpteenth time. I also bought some sugar-free, kind-to-teeth, gluten-free fruit gums. This time, this all-natural diet would work. It had to.

11

DÉJÀ-VU

HAVING A FAMILY LIFE AND MY WORK WITH African Perspectives might have healed me. But I had the scars, which have sharpened my intuition. I continued with life: family, work, loyal friends, good food, full-bodied red wine, long walks through the parks of Maastricht, massages, and relaxing oxygen facials. I started writing what had been dubbed 'Ewurabena's Ghana story' in The Hague circles. A colleague advised me to instead write about my professional experiences.

'Don't write about that ridiculous story. You have so much to share from your longstanding demonstrable commitment to human rights and international justice,' she said.

I certainly did not wish to relive the Ghana experience. Yet how could I write about my professional experiences – the violations and intersectional discriminations – without telling my own story? Perhaps I could do both.

The opportunity presented itself after the first ICC Review Conference, when two African women vying for high-profile international justice positions in The Hague were duly elected at the UN Headquarters in New York. I even found myself involved in a vigorous campaign for the candidate for one of the positions, at the ICC. Significantly, however, Julia Sebutinde from Uganda became the first

African woman to join the International Court of Justice, sixty-six years after the Court's establishment. Prior to that, fourteen African men had served on the ICJ. It was a historic first for African women. Sebutinde's election on the 13th of December 2011 and swearing-in in 2012 took me back to my first visit to the Peace Palace in The Hague, the seat of the International Court of Justice, in 1990. There were no women there, not until Rosalyn Higgins' election in 1995, a historic first for women. I started writing *Hague Girls* in 2012 to include my Ghana story. But my story got in the way. It kept coming up even as I was telling other stories, and so I decided to dedicate a separate chapter to that and tell my story once and for all. That chapter turned out to be this book: *Hague Girls Part One: Fleeing.*

I attended the ICC Review Conference in Kampala, Uganda in 2010. As I was waiting to check in to enter the premises of the conference, I recognised a tall man who was about to join the long queue. I had met him seven years earlier, during the election of the first ICC judges at the UN Headquarters in New York. He looked in my direction. After my 'Ghana experience', I was not too keen to hobnob with Ghanaian officials. My compatriot must have sensed that I was trying to avoid him, but nonetheless walked straight towards me until I could no longer do so. He was carrying a copy of African Perspectives' clean-cut and colourful quarterly journal. He must have attended the workshop we convened the previous day and bought his copy there. We also held a forum after our workshop attended by four hundred participants, including university students, in Uganda. Our meetings had been packed with a diverse range of participants – the *crème de la crème* of international criminal justice, including ICC Prosecutor Luis Moreno Ocampo; Deputy Prosecutor Fatou Bensouda; UN Assistant Secretary-General Adama Dieng, who would later become UN Under-Secretary-General for the Prevention of Genocide; Christian Wenaweser, President of the Assembly of States Parties to the ICC; Professor Leila Sadat, Chairperson of the Crimes Against Humanity Initiative; Jutta Bertram-Nothnagel, Director of Relations with Inter-governmental Organisations, International Association of Lawyers; Judge Elizabeth Ibanda-Nahamya of the International Crimes Division of the High Court of Uganda; and indeed Ambassador Mirjam Blaak of Uganda, who is to be credited for the first Review Conference having taken place on African soil. She suggested that Uganda host the Review Conference, bringing the Court closer to victims of war crimes and crimes against humanity. She and her Ugandan colleagues succeeded against all odds, as there were many countries that did not want Uganda to host the Review Conference. There were also those who did not want to travel to Africa, having to take the malaria prophylaxis and get their jabs. Ambassador Blaak and her colleagues did a lot of lobbying and eventually won the consensus.

Judge Fatoumata Dembélé Diarra, First Vice President of the International Criminal Court; Betty Kaari Murungi, the Africa Representative of the Board of ICC Trust Fund for Victims; Gabrielle McIntyre of the International Criminal Tribunal for the Former Yugoslavia; Carla Ferstman, Director of REDRESS; and Benjamin Ferencz, the last surviving prosecutor of the Nuremberg Trials, were among the *crème de la crème* at the Review Conference itself. Ministers of justice of ICC member states attended, as did representatives of non-member states. The list of magnificent women attending the Conference included Brigid Inder of the Women's Initiatives for Gender Justice; Lorraine Smith van-Lin, who ran the ICC Programme of the International Bar Association; and Ottilia Anna Maunganidze of the Institute for Security Studies.

'Ewurabena, I am sorry about what happened to you in Ghana,' said my compatriot, who was Ghana's ambassador to a political and diplomatic capital, when he came up to me at the Conference. What could I say? I was touched by his gesture. 'Do not let Anas get away with this,' he said. 'So, what was this all about? Was the woman just trying to evict you?'

Indeed, this is how Anas got involved: to help the woman accomplish her goal. I told him we had had a tenancy dispute. African Perspectives had moved out of her premises, and she was not happy about it. She had sued, and her suit had been dismissed. So, she tried to take it out on me personally. I told him the woman was the wife of General Bonsu.

'Anas has defamed me before, you know,' he said.

I needed a minute to try and digest this revelation. Anas, the award-chasing reporter, who apparently enjoys government support, maybe even works for the current government, had libelled this long-serving civil servant and senior diplomat. 'What did he do? What did he falsely accuse you of?' I asked.

The diplomat told me it was during his tenure as Director of Passports at the Ministry of Foreign Affairs in Accra. He believed someone had put Anas up to it. He said he was at work when his wife called him, sobbing. An article Anas had written about him was being discussed on the radio, and a commentator – I did not ask if this commentator was Anas himself or a co-conspirator – had said that the senior diplomat 'ought to be shot by the firing squad'.

Is this what free speech has come to? Imagine a country so free that a perpetrator can go on national radio to incite grave violence. Why were the persons involved not arrested? They would have certainly been detained if the violence had been directed against top politicians or their agents.

The senior diplomat told me he would introduce me to the Minister for Foreign Affairs if he came to the Review Conference. He said he had not seen him yet but had seen the Attorney-General and Minister of Justice, Betty Mould-Idrissu.

'Do you know Betty?' he asked. That question was to be expected; we were both female lawyers, both Ghanaian, and both of us have worked in human rights – the Attorney-General had been Head of the Legal and Constitutional Affairs Division at the Commonwealth Secretariat in London until recently. However, I did not practise partisan politics, nor did I have local political aspirations, whereas Betty had returned to Ghana for a political appointment after her party came back into power in 2009.

I had not met Ghana's first female Attorney-General, but we had known of each other long before her appointment. We had corresponded in the past, and I once published an article she wrote in African Perspectives' quarterly journal. At the beginning of 2009, and shortly after her appointment as Attorney-General, a mutual friend had written to her about our interest in having her officiate at a conference of African Perspectives that was going to be held in Accra. She had responded warmly. Little did I know that I would be brutally libelled and slandered under her watch barely two months later.

The senior diplomat and I made our way into the assembly room. While we were chatting, another Ghanaian civil servant happened to be passing by. I knew him. He had served as Deputy Head of Mission at the Ghanaian Embassy in The Hague. He was also the civil servant who, on behalf of the Minister for Foreign Affairs, had signed the headquarters agreement between the Government of Ghana and African Perspectives. I had not seen or heard from Eric Odoi Anim since our meeting at his home during his tenure in The Hague. On that occasion, I had met with him to discuss the dispute between African Perspectives and the General's wife, because we could not participate in the lawsuit she had initiated due to our headquarters agreement. Eric had previously heard Barbara Bonsu's side of the story and would now hear our side. He concluded that Barbara Bonsu had no claim. However, he pointed out that it was not a good idea to have rented from someone I was acquainted with, which he felt had made the dispute personal. Point taken.

'I knew I would see you here,' he said. Eric could not look me in the eye when he saw me in Kampala, yet he hugged me. He couldn't look me in the eye because when the new government falsely accused African Perspectives of having fraudulently procured the headquarters agreement, he should have come forward to tell the truth, but he hadn't. I of course issued a statement explaining how the agreement came about and who had been involved in the negotiations, with Eric mentioned as the Minister's representative.

As I looked for a place to sit in the designated area for NGOs, I noticed a rather large woman wearing traditional Ghanaian kente clothing, with a huge headgear, sitting at the front of the assembly room. Even though her headgear was the style preferred by Nigerians, she had to be Ghanaian. Not because she was wearing kente, but because of the kind she was wearing and how she wore it. It was not the classic bright, colourful type also preferred by tourists and those in the diaspora. She was wearing the subtle and understated white and grey kente. As I got closer, I realised it was Betty Mould-Idrissu, the Attorney-General and Minister of Justice of Ghana. Just over a year before I would have felt so proud to see a well-attired Ghanaian dignitary in this international setting, but not that day. I recognised a familiar face in her entourage, the Acting Director of Public Prosecutions.

About a year earlier, just months after we left Ghana, I had seen the Acting DPP at an international justice conference in Cape Town. I mentioned the media attacks in my presentation. During the break, the Acting DPP had walked up to me and said, 'Those media men are cruel, they are wicked, they said they would bring us evidence, and up to now we have not seen anything.'

'Shouldn't you take action against them?' I had asked her. 'Should I not have recourse in a democratic country?'

The Acting DPP had responded that Ghana's criminal libel laws had been repealed. She had suggested that I file a complaint with the National Media Commission. As if that would give me any recourse. As if it would bring the perpetrators to justice. Had the National Media Commission and its Chairperson not heard about the widespread allegations? Did they see any evidence confirming those allegations? Had they not read about my widely publicised suit against the perpetrators? And had they not read about the defendants' desperate attempts to have the suit dismissed? Would the defendants not have welcomed the suit if they had the evidence to prove their wild allegations?

'But you just said that what they did was cruel,' I had replied to the Acting DPP. 'And I must say that their cruelty was widespread, throughout the Ghanaian media and on the internet. People all over the world could read their brutal and hateful accusations.'

However, the Acting DPP had hinted that she would not get permission to prosecute from her boss, the Attorney-General. Even if she had not been Acting DPP and was the permanent officeholder, she would not have had the authority to prosecute. The nature of the offence clearly suggested that the government or its officials had a hand in it and the perpetrators were likely acting with the government's favour.

Back at the Review Conference in Kampala, I went up to the Ghanaian delegation. 'Hello, my ex-compatriots,' I said, standing face to face with Betty Mould-Idrissu. She looked confused. She did not recognise me, and that was to be expected because we had never met, nor was I a public figure. The general Ghanaian public had not heard my name before the defamation.

'My name is Ewurabena,' I said.

'Ewurabena, you made some of us lose sympathy for you,' she said. Indeed, from reports I'd got, she had not been sympathetic at all. I had been naïve to think that a female Attorney-General would not tolerate such brutal, widespread, and gendered media assaults.

'Why? Is it because I had a dispute with a general's wife?' I asked.

'I hope you are not going to cause any problems here,' she replied. She probably thought I was about to take to the podium, help myself to the microphone, and announce my experience in Ghana to the delegates who were taking their seats in the assembly hall. 'Why didn't you come and see me? It was a question of interpretation,' she said, referring to the headquarters agreement and its abrupt termination. According to reliable sources, the abrupt termination of the headquarters agreement was in response to my suit against the media men. They thought that by causing a national commotion in the media, I would be forced to submit to the demands of the General's wife, on a matter that was before a court of law.

Indeed, they had not expected me to sue when the brothel allegations broke. They had expected me to go and see them – the Ghanaian way. And now the Attorney-General was asking why I had not gone to see her. Why had they not asked to see me before the attacks or even after the attacks? The thought of going to see the new government officials did not even cross my mind. At some point, it became clear to me that the government, or at least people with the state apparatus at their disposal, were involved. I've worked in international criminal justice long enough to know that such widespread media mayhem does not occur unabated without the government's involvement or blessing. Not to trivialise the Holocaust in Nazi Germany or the genocide in Rwanda, but in all those cases, the media was used as a weapon of war against innocent people. Besides, had I not grown up in a coup-prone Ghana where the media was used by coup plotters?

'I had left the country,' I told the Attorney-General. Not that I would have gone to see her if I had still been there.

'No, you were still in the country,' she insisted. How would she know? Were they keeping tabs on my movement? Well, if so, then they got it wrong. We had left the country as soon as there was good reason to believe that the government was involved.

'What about the media accusations that I was running a brothel?' I asked the Attorney-General.

'I did not hear about that,' she said. Of course she hadn't.

I did not tell her that I knew about the conversations she had had with a senior official at the Ghana Commission for Human Rights and Administrative Justice, or her utterances to Professor Richard Turkson, or her 'cagey' response to Professor Thuso Mundo, an international law scholar who had called her to ask what was going on in Ghana when the media attacks erupted.

In fact, I only found out much later that Thuso, a US-based African scholar, had intervened upon the prompting of a mutual friend. I was touched when I learned that our mutual friend had called Thuso to tell him, 'Ewurabena is being attacked in Ghana. We have to mobilise.' Thuso would later tell me that he had called the Attorney-General, whom he knew, to find out why I was being attacked. He said her response had been cagey. She simply said, 'I am not the one dealing with it.'

The Attorney-General also did not know that I knew of her tête-à-tête with Professor Richard Turkson at the function where Obama addressed the Ghanaian Parliament and that he had brought up our headquarters agreement with her. She had responded agitatedly, 'It was fraudulently procured. This whole thing has become so political; I'll wash my hands of it.' She must have been surprised that a respected member of their party was speaking on behalf of African Perspectives. Professor Turkson told her gently but firmly that the agreement was not fraudulently procured and that the false allegations should be corrected. She then made a one hundred and eighty degree change in position: 'It was not fraudulently procured,' she admitted.

African Perspectives had issued a press statement explaining the background of the agreement, who had been involved in its conclusion, and who had known about it. If the government officials and their collaborators in the media were genuine and acting in good faith, they would have conducted an investigation, and I would have welcomed it. They would have questioned me and other representatives of African Perspectives. They would have questioned those that were named in our press statement, among them Eric Odoi Anim, the official from the Ghana Foreign Affairs who had signed the agreement on behalf of the previous government's Foreign Minister, and his colleague who had witnessed his signature. If the relevant officials in the new government were acting in good faith, they would have asked Ghana Supreme Court Justice Sophia Akuffo, who had witnessed the agreement on behalf of African Perspectives, if she had indeed done so. They would have asked the previous Foreign Minister, Nana Akufo-Addo, if he had known about the agreement. But of course they didn't.

The Attorney-General also did not know that I had been informed about the conversation she'd had with the Commission for Human Rights and Administrative Justice, in which she had said that there was no basis for such an agreement. Actually, there was, but perhaps she simply did not know. Even if we were to assume for a moment that there was no basis for such an agreement, does it mean that it was fraudulently procured?

She had also commented to the Commission for Human Rights and Administrative Justice that there was nothing on record about the negotiations for the headquarters agreement. If this was true, then it had nothing to do with me or African Perspectives but rather the relevant ministries' filing and archiving system. We had our copy of the headquarters agreement and we made it available to those interested.

The Commission for Human Rights and Administrative Justice had reportedly addressed the brothel allegations with the Attorney-General because they believed that an injustice had been done to me. The Attorney-General reportedly said that because the Foreign Minister had got involved, it would be difficult for her office to intervene. In other words, if they were to take on the perpetrators, the Foreign Minister would be implicated. More specifically, the Attorney-General could not take on another member of the same government.

What did the Attorney-General mean when she said that I made some of them lose sympathy for me? She was at least acknowledging that something terrible had happened, that an injustice had been done to me. So why did some people supposedly lose sympathy for me? Was she referring to my open letter to Barack Obama, written after he endorsed Anas?

When the perpetrators reproduced my letter to Obama – which had been posted on African Perspectives' website – through one of their media allies, along with insults directed at me, and in violation of the High Court injunction against them, I got an unexpected message from a former Ghanaian ambassador whom I'd known some time ago when he was stationed in The Hague as deputy head of mission. He'd sent a message to African Perspectives asking the recipient to 'please tell Ewurabena to call her old friend, Ambassador Kofi Daddey.' In fact, he had known about the headquarters agreement and my interactions with Eric Odoi Anim on the agreement. I did speak with Ambassador Daddey after I received his message. It was hard to hear him on the call. Why was he only calling now and not when the attacks began? I suspected it was an official call. Had the Foreign Minister put him up to it? During our conversation, he said, 'No one who knows you will believe those stories.' Did he express those sentiments to the Foreign Minister, Alhaji Mumuni? What about the masses who did not know me; would they believe those stories?

A couple of years later, Betty Mould-Idrissu, then the Minister for Education, was mentioned in a widely publicised 'gargantuan corruption scandal' that had happened during her tenure as Attorney-General and Minister of Justice. She was required to resign from office. It is difficult to form an opinion on this because there's so much that is politicised in Ghana. I recognised another name amongst those implicated in the scandal: none other than Paolo, the developer in the community where we purchased our home. There were constant calls on the airwaves for Paolo and Betty's arrest, amongst others. There were media reports that Paolo had fled to his native country in southern Europe. However, residents of the gated community believed he had gone to England. As for Betty, I don't think she had much to fear. This was, after all, her party in power, even if she had been made to resign from office. Moreover, she had the right connections in Ghanaian politics, regardless of which party was in government. I read that she wrote a statement responding to those allegations and personally went to hand it to the police. Paolo stayed out of Ghana for a long time, eventually returning when things quietened down.

Privately I wondered if the former Attorney-General knew Paolo well, in view of both of them having allegedly been implicated in this gargantuan scandal. Did she know that I had been in litigation with Paolo about our property in the gated community?

At the ICC Review Conference in Kampala, I felt a sense of déjà-vu. The feeling had nothing to do with the fact that this beautiful and scenic city on seven hills reminded me of another Garden of Eden, Kigali in Rwanda. Nor did it have anything to do with the fact that both Uganda and Rwanda have experienced atrocities and untold suffering. During an earlier visit to Kampala, I was told that the grounds of the splendid hotel where I stayed were home to many a human skull and had been one of the locations where the remains of the victims of former President Idi Amin were dumped. The story had reminded me of a visit to the genocide memorial sites in Rwanda, where the skulls and faces of beautiful Tutsi women with long hair, sometimes wearing glasses, were on display. There must have been men too, but it was the remains of the women that stuck in my mind. How could such anguish have occurred in the green, fertile and gorgeous territories of Rwanda and Uganda?

The sense of déjà-vu instead came during the opening ceremony of the Review Conference. It took me back to my encounter with blatant gender discrimination at the Tenth Session of the African Commission on Human and Peoples' Rights in Banjul, almost two decades earlier. It was my first session at the African Commission. I was surprised to observe that each of the Commission's eleven members were men. Was I the only one who noticed this? How was this even possible at the level of a human rights protection body? I was attending the Commission's session from Minnesota and was not quite sure if this blatant disparity was the accepted norm in Africa. I thought to myself, 'Well, I am not going to say anything. Perhaps this is how things are done here, so first observe.' After all, I was there as an observer. Many people, both men and women, were in attendance. Some of them had attended previous meetings of the Commission and it was not up to me to start raising objections about the African Commission's all-male membership. There were quite a few forceful women present, as well as outspoken men, and so I was not about to open my mouth on this gender inequality. I felt embarrassment for the men on the panel and wondered whether they were not ashamed to sit on what appeared to be a sexist body.

I was so relieved when a rather smallish African man, Meshack, spoke up. He appeared larger than his slight frame when he criticised the total absence of women on the Commission. Meshack was representing an academic institution in Sweden, where he lived. He told the participants that he was in exile because of human rights. He used to teach law in his native Kenya and had been forced out of the country during the government's clampdown on academics accused of teaching 'subversive activities'. I would later learn that his house was burned down amidst those accusations. More than two decades later, he was vindicated, along with others, and given a symbolic compensation.

Why had the women, including me, not spoken up about the absence of women on the eleven-member Commission? Certainly, other women must have noticed this obvious omission or exclusion and must have been concerned about it too. So why did we not speak up? Because change would eventually come, and we did not want to have burned our bridges before it did. African states were not likely to nominate women who they deemed aggressive or troublemakers to an international court or quasi-international court – or a national court for that matter. Looking back, I believe if I had been in a similar setting amongst Africans and non-Africans in a western society, I would not have had difficulty speaking up, even if it cost me some friends. However, in this African setting I was not quite sure what else it would cost me, so I kept quiet.

I was in my twenties, ambitious and determined. Apart from my African last name, I appeared quite westernised in many other respects. I was at the session representing an American lawyers' group, I was about to be married to my Dutch boyfriend, and I was not exactly conservative in the way I dressed. A Ghanaian man attending the session would say to me, 'Ewurabena, you are an un-strategic dresser. If you want to be taken seriously you should dress differently.' I wore trousers and short skirts; I think I looked good. Only once did I wear a white blouse that was see-through from the back – not strategic indeed.

But I did take myself seriously. That is why I would later write a pioneering book on the African Commission and found African Perspectives. Researchers and scholars who would later study the Commission tell me mine was one of the few works available on the Commission at that time. I had studied the African Charter on Human and Peoples' Rights, the treaty that established the African Commission. I don't recall reading anywhere that the members of the Commission were all male, perhaps because the articles available on the Charter were also written by men – African, European and American. What I found fascinating was President Léopold Sédar Senghor's charge to the African jurists who gathered in Dakar, Senegal in 1979 to begin work on the first draft of the African Charter. He said: 'Europe and America have construed their systems of rights and liberties, with reference to a common civilization, and specific aspirations. It is not for us Africans either to copy them or seek originality for originality's sake. It is for us to manifest both imagination and skill. Those of our traditions that are positive may inspire us. You should therefore constantly keep in mind our values and the real needs of Africa.'

President Senghor nonetheless cautioned the African experts 'not to produce a Charter on the rights of the African [person], because [hu]mankind is one and indivisible and the basic needs of [human beings] are similar everywhere.'

Those words of wisdom spoke to me and have stayed with me throughout my career. They have contributed to shaping my views on human rights and international justice, in fact, on any topic. Not that I didn't already know that as Africans we need not copy blindly, nor necessarily start from scratch. As an African I wanted to be treated with dignity like my European and American counterparts. Still, seeing those words of a prominent Africanist and internationalist, articulated so well, gave me permission to advance what I already knew and felt.

However, others are more cynical about Senghor's views and didn't think they could be the perspective of Africans. They believed his mind had been neo-colonised by the French. His first name was *Léopold*, for crying out loud. He was even a member of the Académie Française, France's official authority on the use of the French language. How could a person so immersed in French culture, with its corresponding history of colonial assimilation, speak for Africa? Never mind that Senghor was born in Africa, of

Africans, and was President of an African country for two decades.

Could it be that Senghor's exposure to different cultures may have sharpened his perspectives on Africa for the better? Kwesi Mensah, a Ghanaian journalist who was in exile in London during the Rawlings era, explained it best. He said in London he made a point of going to an African church, but in his native Ghana he would simply go to church. In other words, he was more conscious of being an African when he lived in London. As for me, I am not sure I would have been so preoccupied with African perspectives on human rights and international justice if I did not have other perspectives and attitudes to compare them with on a regular basis. I might not have concerned myself with African perspectives on various issues if I had lived in Ghana most of my adult life and surrounded myself with colleagues and family members whose outlooks were mostly similar to mine – but maybe I would have.

At my first session of the Commission, how would a seemingly progressive intervention by me be perceived? Was I even in a position to speak for the women of Africa? My westernisation might have been used against me.

After Meshack called upon the Commission to have a membership that reflects the African populace, two of the Commission's members had some interesting things to say. The first one started his response with, 'I love women,' and then went on to inform participants about how, as Attorney-General of his country, he was being sued by a female lawyer alleging that the country's nationality laws discriminated against women. The other member expressed the view that it was not up to the Commission itself to advocate for inclusion of female members. He said it was up to the States Parties, who nominate candidates for the Commission, who are then elected by the African Union Assembly. Then he dropped a bomb. He said if the all-male members of the Commission were to raise this issue with Africa's heads of state and justice ministers, the Commission's intentions would be misconstrued: African leaders might think that the members of the Commission wanted female members amongst them to keep them from getting bored as they deliberate human rights in Africa.

However, Meshack's intervention about the absence of women on the Commission did have an impact. Now that he had exposed the elephant in the room, others began to call for the inclusion of women on the Commission. In fact, the African Commission took it upon itself to advocate for inclusion of female members when a position became vacant. Cape Verde nominated Vera Duarte and she was duly elected to the Commission. It was a historic first for African women. She went on to become Vice-Chair of the Commission, and since her election many more women have joined the Commission. Sometimes the female members have outnumbered the male members, and women have served as Chair.

Twenty years later, at the ICC Review Conference in Kampala, seated in the front row of the high table before us in the assembly room were the heads of state of Tanzania and Uganda; heads of intergovernmental bodies; the current and former Secretaries-General of the United Nations, Ban Ki-moon and Kofi Annan; the President and Prosecutor of the ICC, Judge Sang-Hyun Song and Luis Moreno Ocampo, and other notable dignitaries. They were all men. Seated behind these important men were their supporters, their deputies, and the like – the women. It reminded me of images in a post-colonial African setting, where the women rally behind their men, cheering them on, supporting their candidacy for office. It's still a man's world.

ACKNOWLEDGEMENTS

Belated thank you to my beloved mother, Elizabeth Esi Etsuaba of blessed memory, who stood up for me in court, whenever my name was called, in the suit I initiated against the media men. My profound gratitude to gender literary expert Dr Pinkie Mekgwe for having given language to my 'nightmare of media rape'. My heartfelt thanks to Professor Leila Sadat for her support and objectivity. How many people could have written to a newly elected President Barack Obama, like she did, to draw his attention to the fact that the man he praised in his 'message to Africa' was a defendant I had in court in a much-publicised defamation action? Gracias to Desmond Davies for his integrity and professionalism. Dessie, I pray the next generation of African journalists will be inspired by your sincerity.

I owe a debt of gratitude to my tiny editorial team – your compassion and help in bringing this book to fruition made what would otherwise have been an unbearable task enjoyable at times. I can't even begin to fathom what life after political violence and 'media rape' would be like without the unwavering support of friends, family and colleagues. My eternal gratitude to you all, including the women and men I've worked with from the human rights and international justice landscape – those who knew my 'Ghana story' and those who didn't.

ACKNOWLEDGEMENTS

To my gorgeous ladies – I thank you for having adapted so well after our impromptu move. You're fun, you're smart, and did I remember to add gorgeous? And finally, to my dear husband: you did not choose to move to Ghana, and you certainly could not have anticipated those attacks. Thanks for your enduring support, and for having handled it all with grace, perception and insight.

This is the book I had to write, not the one I wanted to write. It has not been easy to relive the 'Ghana experience'. But it would have been well worth it if you, dear reader, have found it a good read. Let it also be a call for truth and justice.

I would love to hear from you. www.haguegirls.com